Welcome to my little book of for kind and loving pet

I LOVE YOU MORE THAN BACON

STARLETT

Menu

Introduction
Starlett's Sprinkles
Great British Breakfasts
Mighty Meaty Meals
Something Fishy
Festive Feasts
Tempting Treats
Afternoon Tea
Feeling Pawly?
Useful Information

INTRODUCTION

When looking into the ingredients listed in commercial pet food you will find a vast majority of them contain meat derivatives and fillers such as corn and other cereals. All of which have no nutritional value and may even cause allergies. When Starlett was a very young puppy I fed her a top of the range pet food which is recommended by Vets. The food contained a huge amount of corn which resulted in Starlett getting very itchy skin, particularly on the insides of her ears. I researched skin allergies in pets and then obviously I stopped giving her this brand of food. Plus, why give your pet something to eat that you would not eat yourself?

I then began feeding her a brand containing healthy organic meat with a little fruit, vegetables and mixed herbs within.

This brand was very high in quality but would work out expensive for a dog with a normal appetite.
Starlett eats well, but very small portions at a time. This food therefore did not stay fresh for very long.

Starlett's diet consists mostly of roast chicken and rice with healthy mixed herbs and sometimes spices. What she really loves is a teaspoon of warm melted coconut oil mixed in well with her food. It actually costs me less to feed her healthy human grade fresh meat as opposed to tinned dog food. Starlett will sometimes eat dried kibble. A small handful of a good quality brand, in chicken with salmon oil flavour which she shares with the local cats.

As West Highland Terriers are a breed prone to having itchy or dry skin conditions, it is vital that their diets contain a little amount of oil. Around 1 teaspoon per day should be enough to do the trick!

When introducing your pet to a new type of food, do it a little sample at a time to ensure it suits them well.

A HEALTHY DOG WILL HAVE :
bright eyes, glossy coat, firm stools and plenty of energy!

DRY FOOD

Many pet owners choose to feed their pet dry food as it is less messy and it remains fresher for longer. However, if your pet is fed dry food "kibble" only they will need to be drinking a good amount of fresh drinking water in order to prevent dehydration.

RAW FOOD

Many people nowadays are opting to feed their pet a raw meat diet with the potential benefits being: shinier coats, healthier skin, increased energy and firm stools. Raw meat should be defrosted in your refridgerator or in your microwave oven. All areas touched by raw meat should be disinfected in order to prevent bacteria growth.

* NEVER GIVE YOUR PETS COOKED BONES AS THEY SPLINTER *

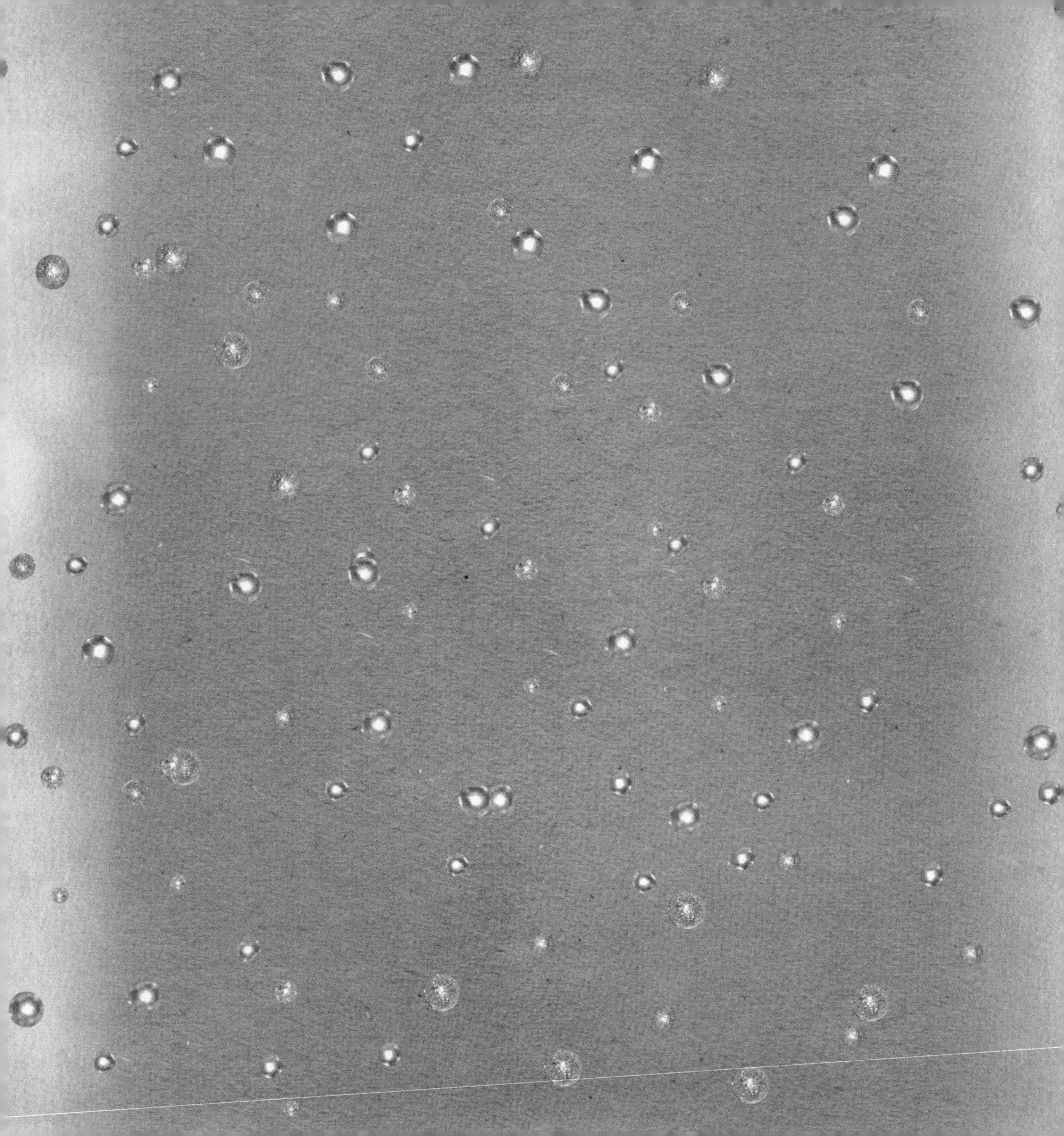

Starlett's Secret Sprinkles

Starlett's Secret Sprinkles are a unique blend of mixed herbs which help to promote optimum health benefits for your pet. Starlett has just a "pinch" "sprinkled" over food each day. The mix contains the following:

ALFALFA: A phytonutrient which aids energy, for healthy joints, mental agility, helps to freshen breath. An antioxident with cancer fighting properties.

ANISEED: Aids the digestive system and thus eases colic pain. Can help to loosen phelgm and ease coughing.

BASIL: Inhibits the growth of bacteria, An anti-inflammatory which is subsquently good for rheumatic and arthritic conditions. Good for the heart as it aids bloodflow and circulation.

BURDOCK ROOT: A blood cleanser and purifer. A great tonic for both the liver and the kidneys.

CELERY SEEDS: Helps to aid with the accumulation of furic acid required for joint health. Calms the digestive system. Relieves gas and associated cramps and also helps with healing urinary tract infections.

CHAMOMILE: Calming and soothing properties. Can help to relieve anxiety and help dogs to settle at night.

CHICKWEED: Aids digestion, arthritis, skin irritation and inflammation.

CHICORY ROOT: Provides good bacteria to the gut and is a probiotic which encourages good health.

CLEAVERS: Good for cleansing the lymphatic system. A rich source of vitamin C. Soothes itchy skin.

DANDELION ROOT: Dandelion primarily aids good liver function. This herb supports the healthy functioning of all other organs.

GOLDEN ROD: Keeps the urinary tract healthy. Good for the skin and fur. Has anti-spasmodic qualities and can help to relieve colicky stomach pain.

KELP: Rich in iron which helps to regulate and balance the thyroid function which plays a major role in growth and development and the rate of metabolism. Good for the skin, coat, teeth and nails.

MARIGOLD PETALS: A good antiseptic with healing properties. Good for repairing all internal organs and notably the skin.

MILK THISTLE SEEDS: Eliminate toxins and help to maintain good liver health. Full of antioxidants which help to detoxify the liver for overall good health.

NETTLES:
A valuble phytonutrient which can be a tonic for overall health.

OREGANO:
Helps to combat arthritis. Aids the respiratory (breathing) system. Heals bee or wasp stings.

PARSLEY:
Helps to prevent kidney problems, including kidney stones and diseases of the urinary tract. An anti-inflammatory which aids arthritis.

PASSION FLOWERS: Calming.

PEPPERMINT:
Aids the digestive system and helps to treat tummy upsets.

ROSEHIPS:
Rich in Vitamin C. Aids arthritis.

ROSEMARY:
High in calcium and iron. An antioxidant.

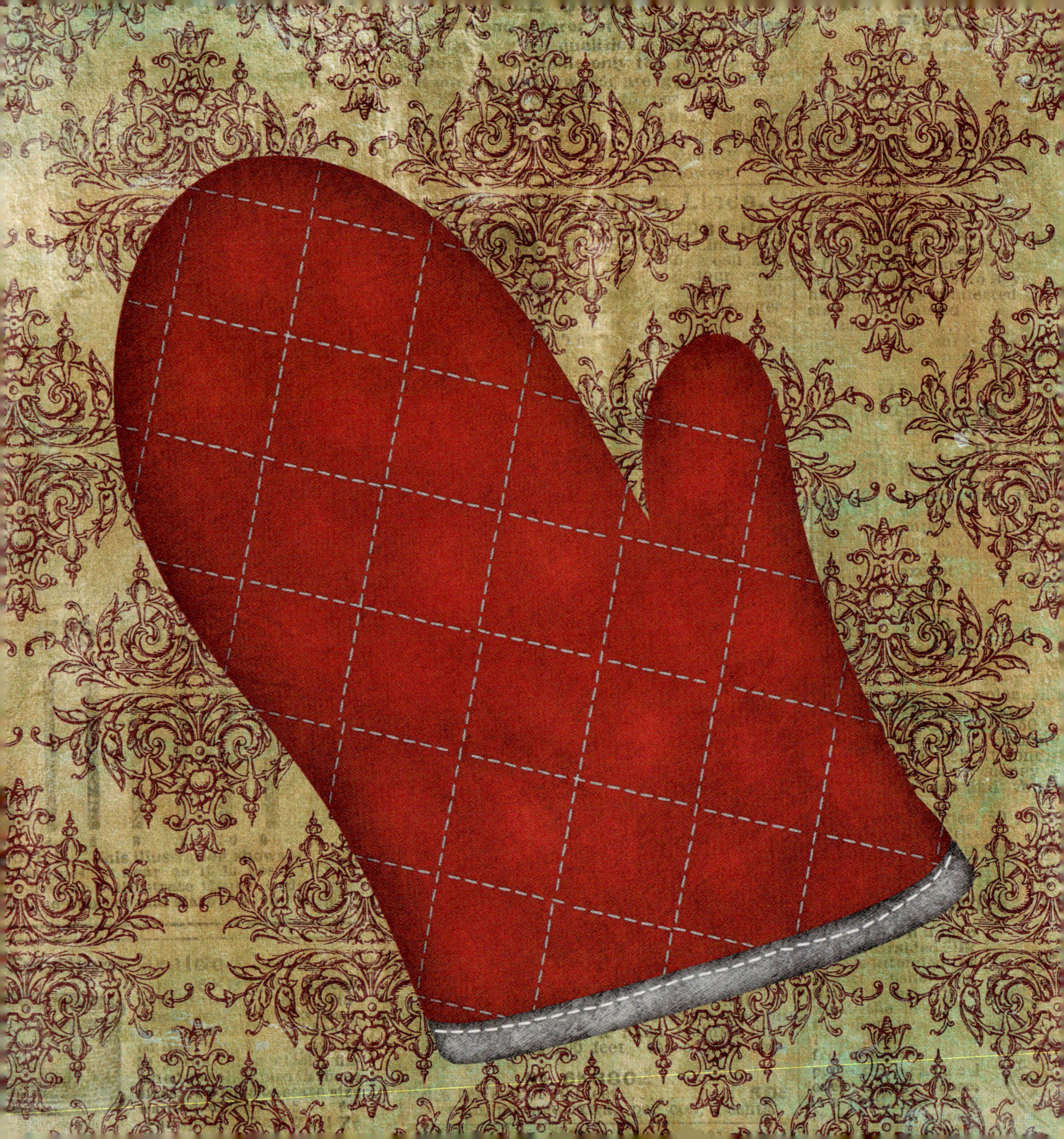

Menu

GREAT BRITISH BREAKFASTS

The Full English

Scrambled Eggs and Herby Ham

Organic Oink Omelette

Perfect Poochy Pancakes

♥

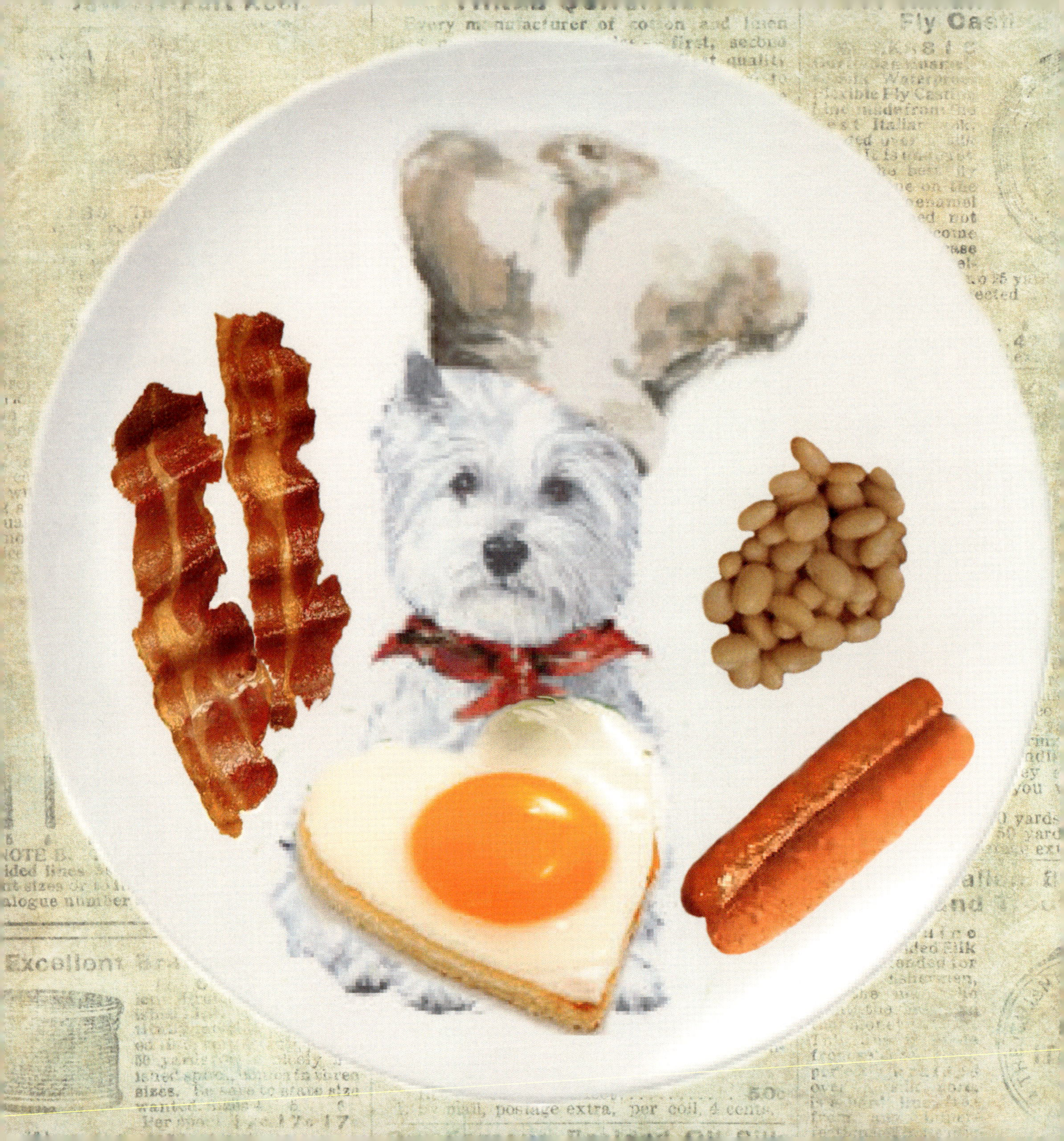

THE FULL ENGLISH

INGREDIENTS

2 slices of streaky bacon
1 low fat sausage, 1 egg
1 tablespoon of baked beans
1/4 slice of toast
1 tablespoon coconut oil

INSTRUCTIONS

Slit your sausage lengthways down its centre to enable it to cook thoroughly and for any unwanted fat to drain out. Bake in your oven alongside your 2 slices of streaky bacon at 375 F for 25 minutes (turning over half way through.)

Meanwhile, wash off the tomatoe sauce from your baked beans, as the excess sugar and salt will not be beneficial. Cook the beans for 1 minute in the microwave.

In a little coconut oil fry your egg, at the same time toast your bread. Then drizzle a few drops of the warm coconut oil on top. Chop it all up in bite-sized pieces, mix and serve.

mixed herbs

SCRAMBLED EGGS AND HERBY HAM

INGREDIENTS

2 eggs
2/3 cup of skimmed milk
1/4 teaspoon of calcium (powdered eggshell)
1 slice of ham
sprinkle of mixed herbs

INSTRUCTIONS

Place the slice of ham on a plate and sprinkle it lightly with the mixed herbs. Roll into a tube shape and chop up.

Break the eggs into a non-stick pan over a medium heat, add the milk and gently stir until it has cooked.

Add in your pre-prepared herby ham and mix it in well.

Pour into your dogs bowl and sprinkle the calcium powder on the top. Cool to room temperature and serve.

STARLETT'S SECRET KITCHEN

ORGANIC OINK OMELETTE

INGREDIENTS

3 tablespoons of olive oil for the frying pan
2 slices of organic bacon
1 organic sausage
mixed herbs
3 eggs

INSTRUCTIONS

In a large pan heat 1 tablespoon of oil and fry the organic bacon and sliced sausage.

Meanwhile beat 3 eggs in a bowl and add in the mixed herbs; mix well.
Chop up the cooked bacon and sausage.
In a separate frying pan, cook the eggs until brown, add in the bacon and sausage. Fold the omelette in half. Allow it to cool and chop it up smaller before serving.

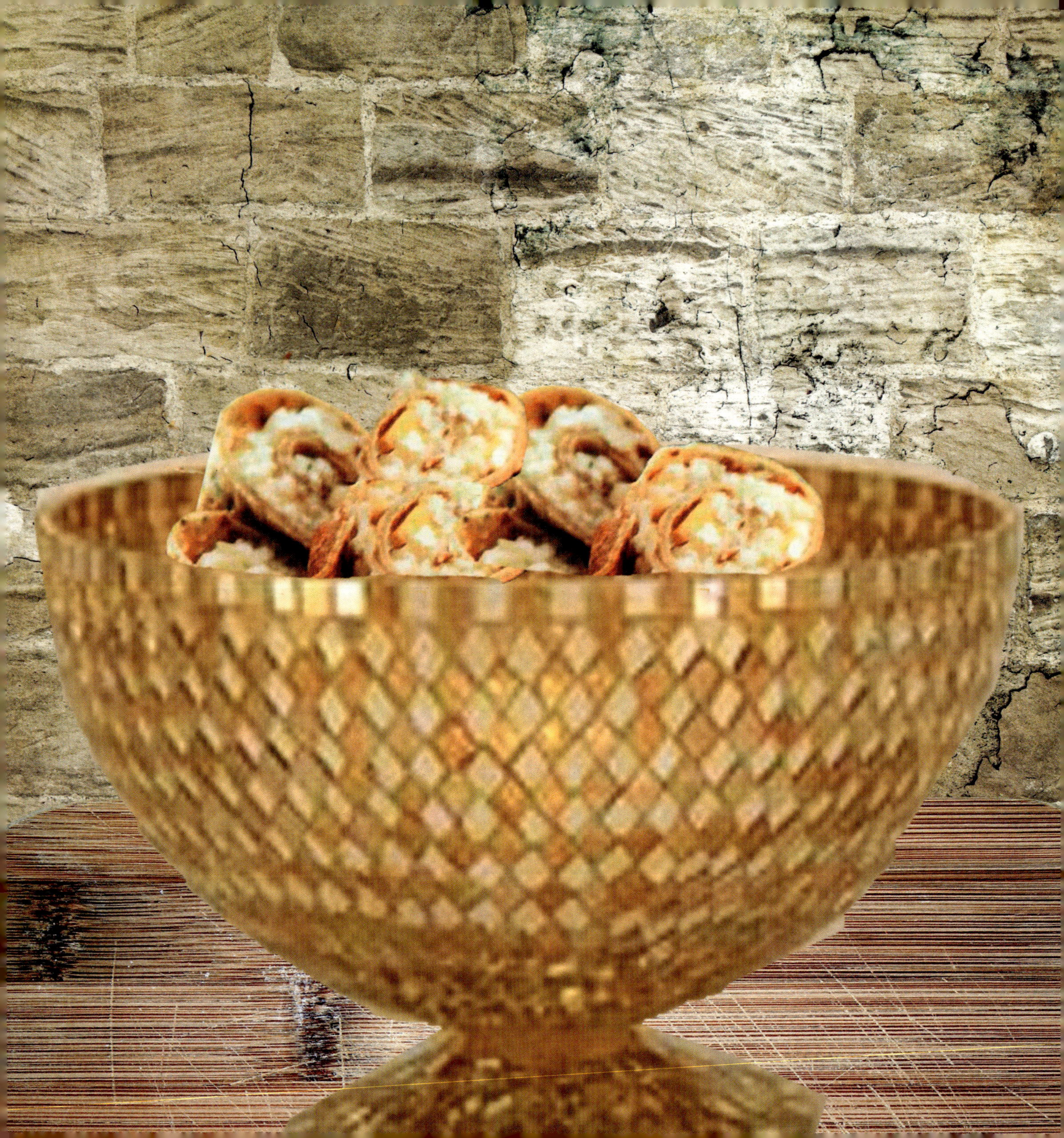

PERFECT POOCHY PANCAKES

INGREDIENTS

For the pancakes:

2 eggs
4oz of whole wheat flour
8 fl oz skimmed milk
1 tablespoon of chopped herbs
vegetable oil for frying

For the filling:

5oz of cottage cheese
1 hard boiled egg (chopped)
1 pureed banana
5oz of cooked rice

INSTRUCTIONS

Mix the flour, eggs and milk to create a batter. Allow to set for 20 minutes and then stir in the chopped herbs.

Fry eight pancakes on a medium heat. Allow them to cool

Mix the cottage cheese, hard boiled egg, banana and rice.

Spread the filling onto the pancakes and roll them up.

Slice them to serve.

THE FONDEST MEMORIES ARE MADE WHEN
gathered around the table.

Menu

MIGHTY MEATY MEALS

Beef Me Up Bowl

Pan-Fried Chicken Delight

Lips Licking Lamb Supreme

Loveable Liver & Bacon Loaf

BEEF ME UP BOWL

INGREDIENTS

7oz of organic minced beef
3oz of mashed potatoes
4 carrots
1 tablespoon of tomato paste
2 tablespoons of coconut oil
16 fl oz of unsalted vegetable stock

INSTRUCTIONS

Peel your carrots and dice them into small cubes. Heat the coconut oil, add in the mashed potatoes and diced carrots and pour in the vegetable stock. Simmer for 20 minutes. Allow to cool and serve.

SPRINKLE ON A FEW MIXED HERBS FOR EXTRA VITAMNS

PAN-FRIED CHICKEN DELIGHT

INGREDIENTS

9 oz (250g) of chicken, 4 potatoes, 2 carrots, 1 courgette, 1 apple, 1 tablespoon of coconut oil, 1 tablespoon of parsley (finely chopped)

INSTRUCTIONS

Dice your carrots and courgettes into small cubes. Peel and dice your potatoes. Place all into a saucepan with 1fl oz of water (300 ml). Bring to the boil and allow to simmer for 20 minutes. Mash it into a rough puree. Dice the chicken and apple into small cubes and brown them in the coconut oil for 20 minutes. Mix this in with the vegetables adding in the parsley.

WILL BE ENJOYED BOTH LUKEWARM OR COLD

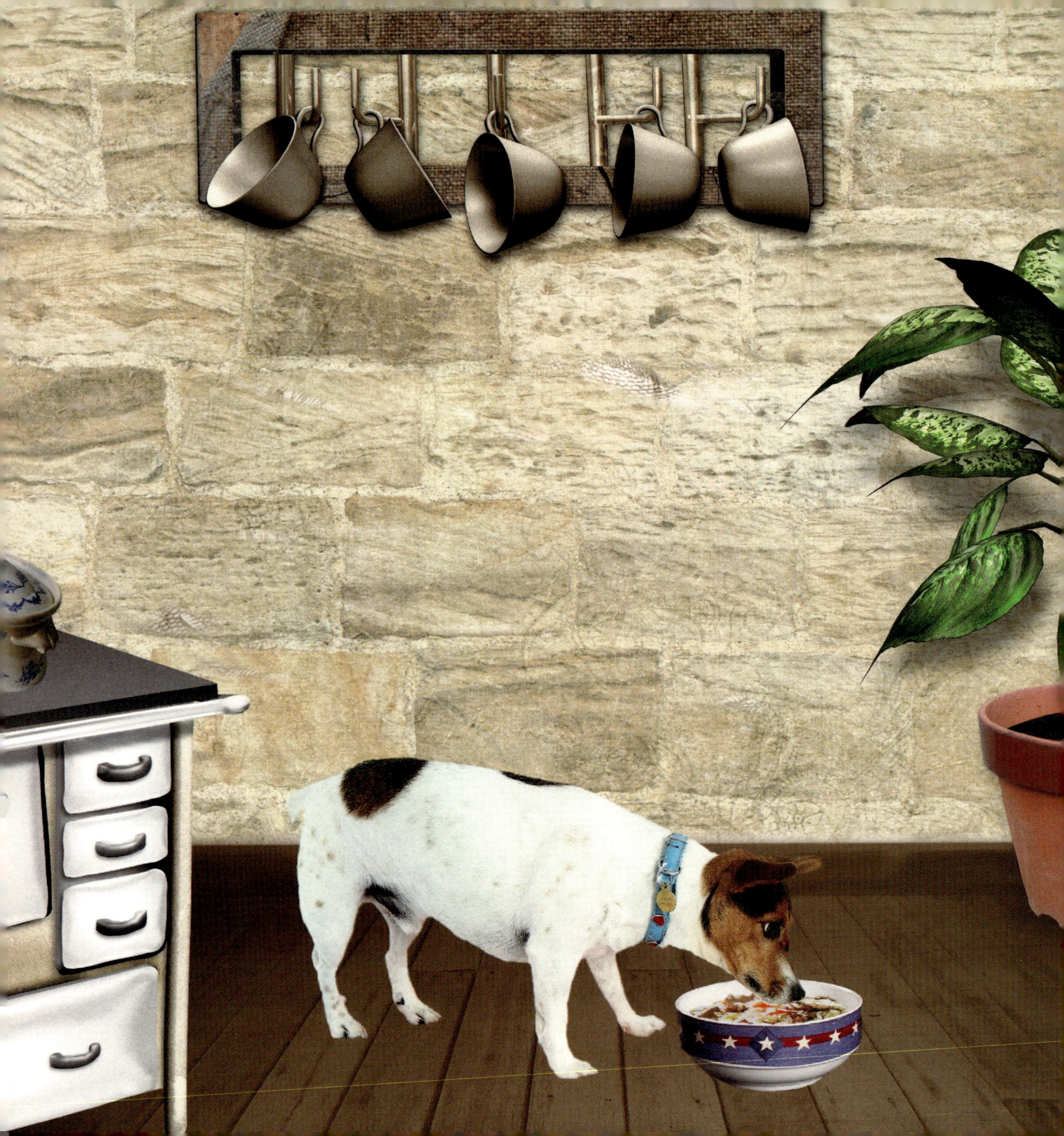

LIPS LICKING LAMB SUPREME

INGREDIENTS

11oz (300g) lamb, 11oz (300g) cooked rice
7oz (200g) swiss chard, 3.5oz (100g) bean sprouts
1 small cooked carrot, 1 hard-boiled egg,
6 fl oz (200ml) unsalted chicken stock
2 sprigs of rosemary, 1 bay leaf, 2 tablespoons olive oil.

INSTRUCTIONS

Dice your lamb and gently brown it in your olive oil. Pour in the chicken stock, add in the rosemary and bayleaf for seasoning, simmer for 25 minutes then take out the herbs.

Chop up the carrot, swiss chard and bean sprouts and add these vegetables together with the cooked rice to the lamb and cook all together for 5 minutes. Sprinkle ontop some chopped hard-boiled egg and serve.

EAT PRAY LOVE

LOVEABLE LIVER & BACON LOAF

INGREDIENTS

500g (18oz) calf's liver, 150g (5oz) breadcrumbs, 2 eggs, 1 packet of low-salt lean bacon, 1 small carrot, 1 celery stalk, 1 red pepper, 1 teaspoon of parsley, 1 teaspoon of sage, 2 tablespoons of coconut oil. 2 tablespoons of flour, 250ml water.

INSTRUCTIONS

Boil your liver in a pan of water for about 10 minutes. Drain off and remove any skin and veins, chop up and press through a sieve. Add the eggs, breadcroumbs, oil and seasonings and mix thoroughly.

Place the mixture in a small loaf tin leaving gaps around the edges. Add 1/2 inch of water and bake for 1 hour at 400F. Place bacon strips over the loaf during the last 20 minutes of baking.
Make gravy using juices left on the bottom of the roasting tin. Mix this with the flour and water. Boil in a pan, stirring well.

CHOP UP THE LOAF AND SERVE WITH THE GRAVY ON TOP

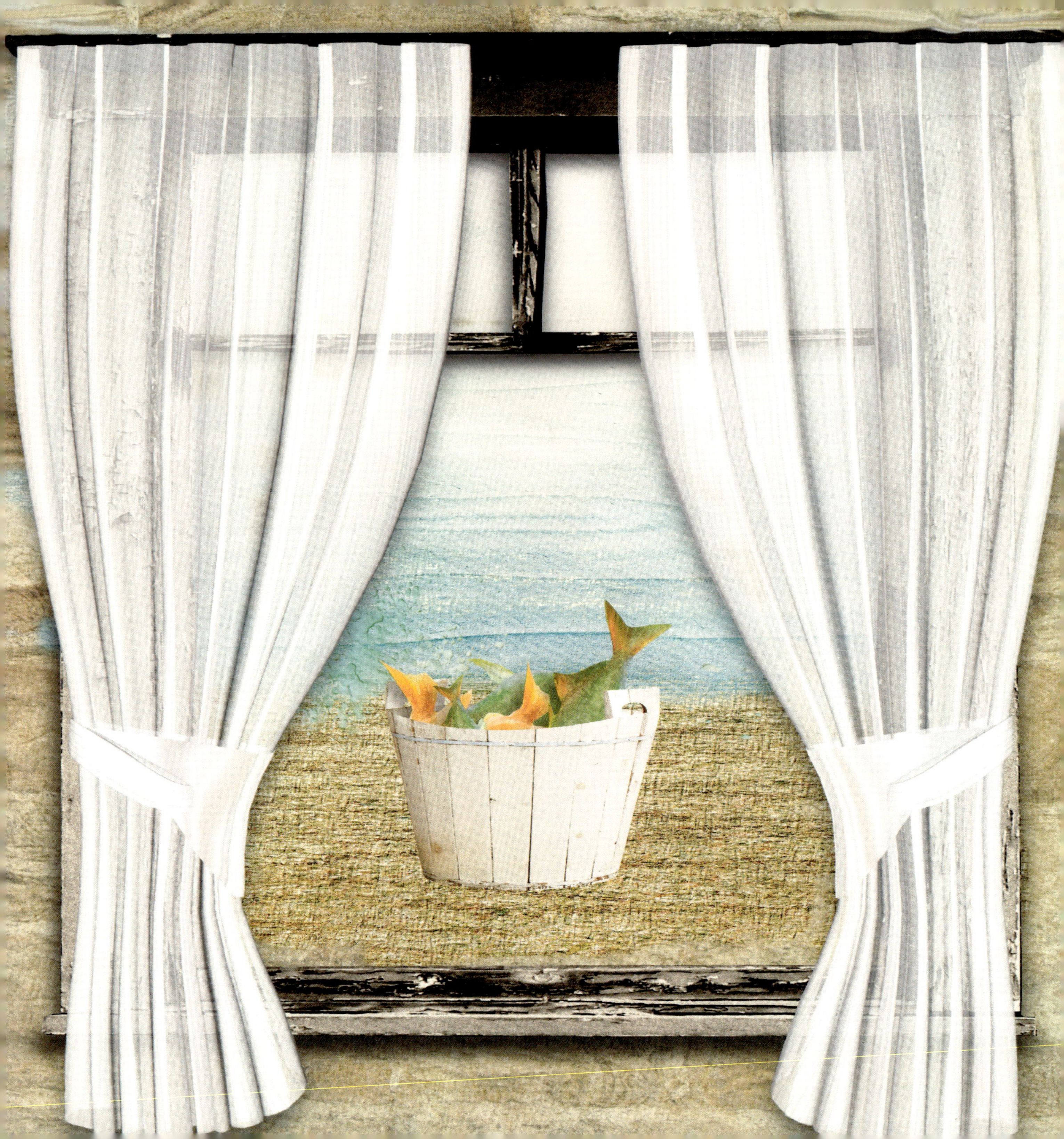

Menu

SOMETHING FISHY

Raw Roar Raw

Salmon & Dill Surprise

Chicken & Tuna Temptation

Clever Cod Stew

♥

RAW ROAR RAW

INGREDIENTS

1 cup of canned mackerel
1 tablespoon of cooked organic brown rice
1 tablespoon of sunflower oil
2 tablespoons of chicken or beef broth

INSTRUCTIONS

Blend together all ingredients until thoroughly mixed together well. Serve to your cat straight away and store any remaining portion in a plastic airtight container in the refridgerator for up to 2-3 days.

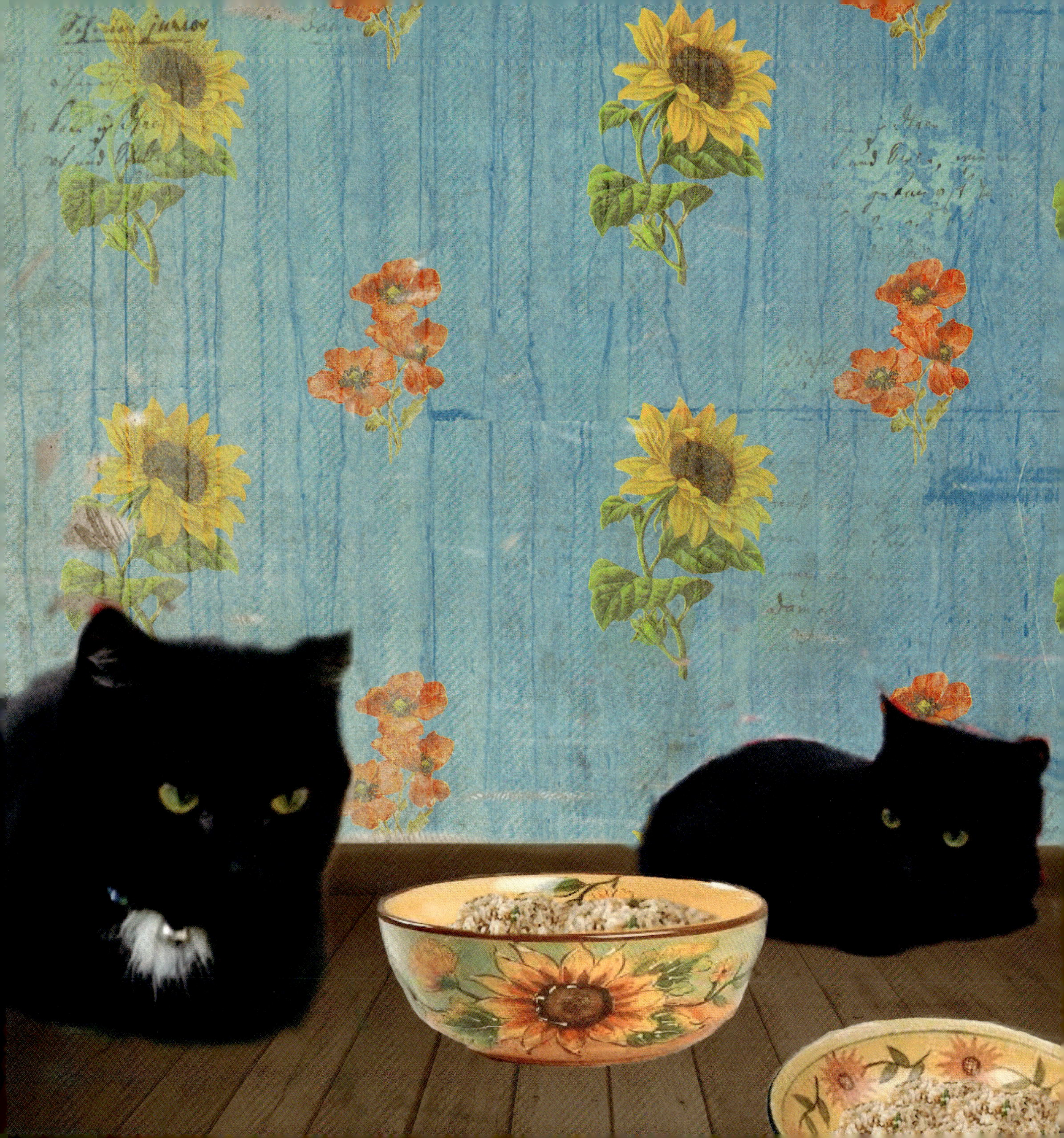

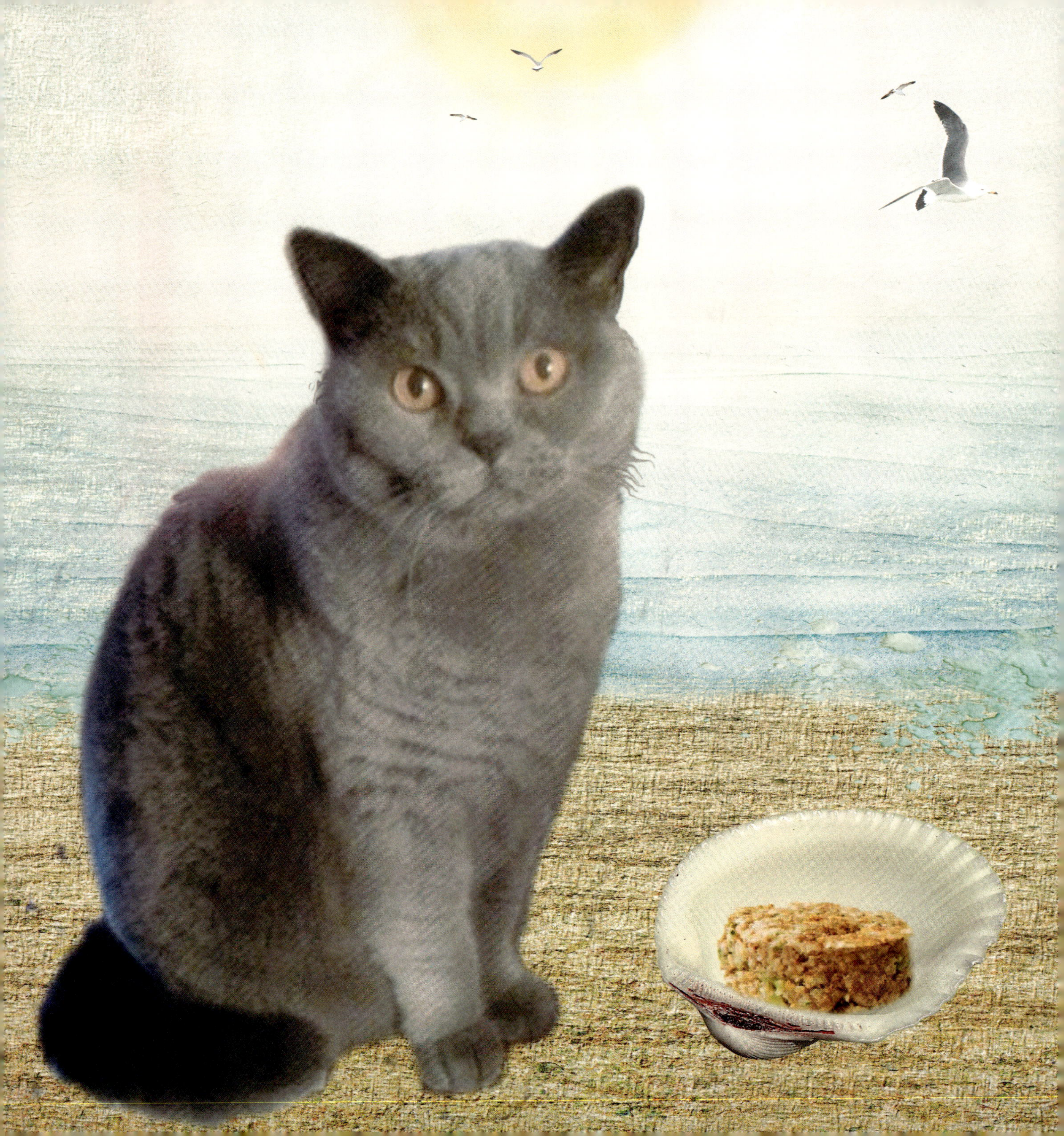

SALMON & DILL SURPRISE

INGREDIENTS

1 can salmon, 1 tablespoon of cooked mashed broccoli, 1/4 cup whole wheat breadcrumbs, 1 teaspoon of dill, 1 teaspoon of brewer's yeast.

INSTRUCTIONS

Combine all of your ingredients in a bowl. Stir together very well and serve cold or warmed up. Keep any leftovers refrigerated, and discard after 3 days.

YOU MAY WISH TO SERVE IT MOLDED INTO A FISH SHAPE OR INSIDE A CUTE SHELL.

You can use fresh salmon if you can afford to.

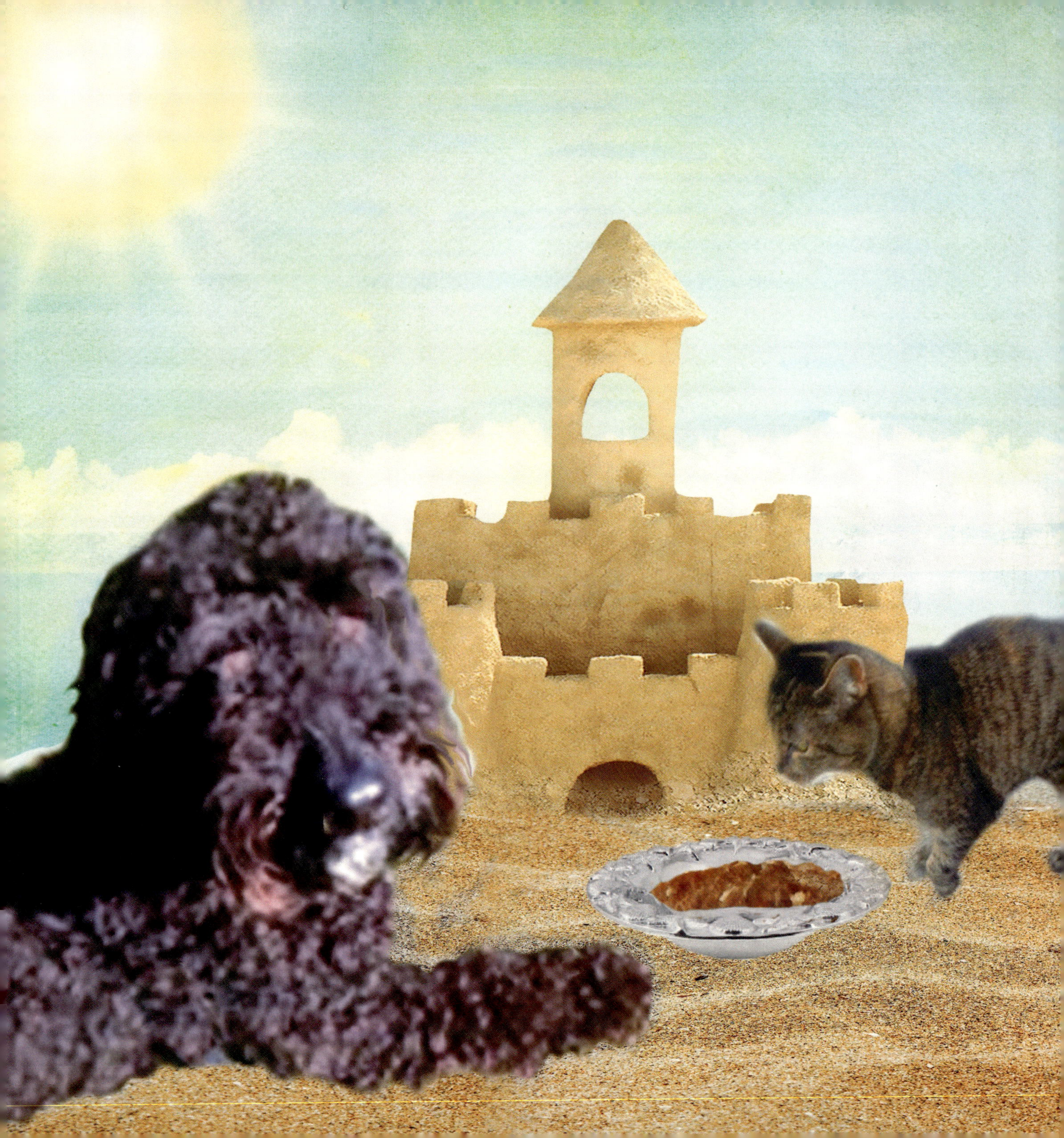

CHICKEN & TUNA TEMPTATION

INGREDIENTS

1/2 cup cooked chicken
1 can of tuna in sunflower oil
1 tablespoon of mashed cooked carrot,
2 tablespoons of brown rice

INSTRUCTIONS

Combine all of your ingredients in a food processor.
Pulse until blended and serve.
Refrigerate leftovers.
Discard after three days.

STARLETT'S
SECRET
OLIVE OIL

CLEVER COD STEW

INGREDIENTS

300g cod fillet (sliced), 250ml water, 200g potatoes (peeled and chopped), 75g green peas, 2 tsp parsley, 2 tsp fresh dill, A pinch of thyme, 2 tsp sea kelp, 1/2 tsp lemon juice and 2 tsp olive oil.

For dog's portion you may wish to add:

2 tsp of bonemeal, 1/2 pear or cantatoupe melon. (chopped).

INSTRUCTIONS

Pour the cold water into your stewing pan then add in your cod, potatoes, peas, parsley, dill and thyme.
Bring to the boil and allow it all to simmer for 8 minutes or until most of the water has been absorbed. Remove from the heat and allow cool. Add in sea kelp, lemon juice and olive oil. Divide into two portions. Add in the bonemeal and chopped pear or cantaloupe melon to dog's portion.

Let's celebrate!

Menu

FESTIVE FEASTS

West Highland Haggis Roast
Birthday Cake
Celebration Muffins
Dog Friendly Easter Egg

Pumpkin Balls
Christmas Pudding

♥

Happy New Year!

WEST HIGHLAND HOGMANAY HAGGIS

INGREDIENTS

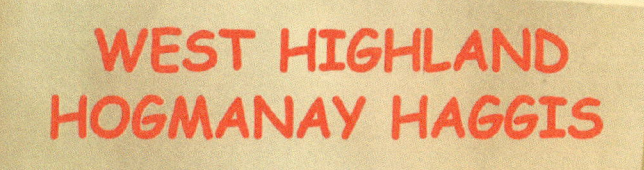

1 roasted sweet potato cut into chunks.
1 whole carrot which has been grated.
1 cup of chopped organic liver, 3/4 cup of red lentils.
1 cup of kidney beans
2 cups of natural chicken stock, 3 cups of Scottish oats,
1 teaspoon of chopped rosemary, a sprinkle of black pepper.

INSTRUCTIONS

Cook the grated carrot in a large saucepan until it is soft. Add in the roasted sweet potato, lentils, liver, oats and chicken stock and bring it to the boil. Allow to simmer for 10 minutes before adding in the kidney beans.

Finally add in your seasoning of chopped rosemary and a sprinkling of black pepper.

Grease 8 muffin tins or a loaf tin, add in mixture and cook in a pre-heated oven at 375F for 30 minutes

ENSURE YOUR ROAST IS COOL BEFORE SERVING

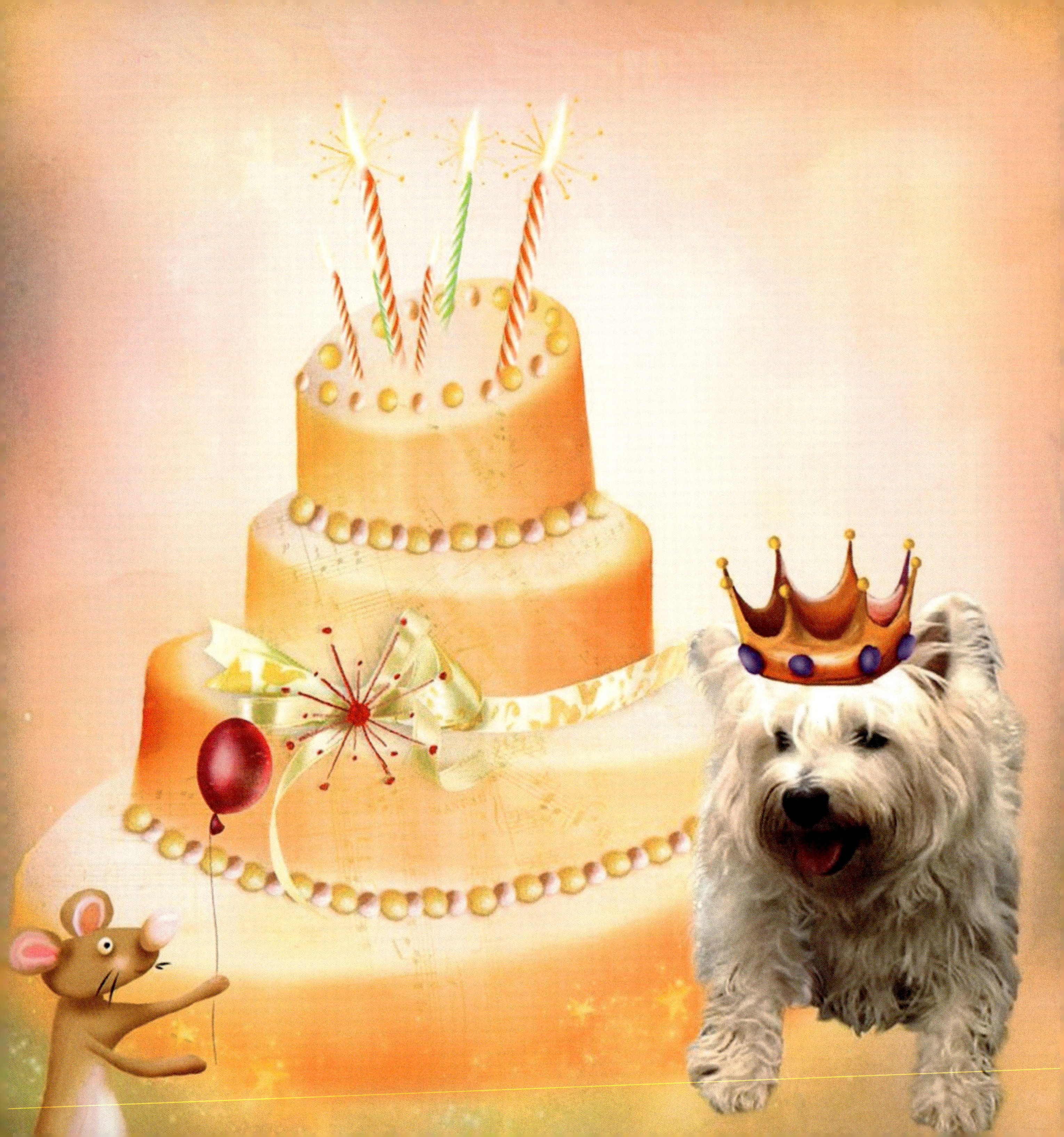

BIRTHDAY CAKE
For Dogs & Humans

INGREDIENTS

1 egg
1/5 cups of wholewheat flour or alternatively white flour
1/4 cup of organic peanut butter (not containing xylitol)
1 carrot which has been shredded
1/4 cup of coconut oil
1/2 cup of apple sauce
1/3 cup of honey
1 teaspoon of vanilla extract
1 teaspoon of baking soda

INSTRUCTIONS

Grease a round tin with coconut oil
In a large mixing bowl, blend together well the egg, peanut butter, oil, vanilla, apple sauce and honey.
Stir in the carrots and mix thoroughly.
Mix together the flour and the baking soda and fold it in to the mixture. Spoon the mixture into the tin.
Cook at 350 (Gas mark 4) for 45 minutes

ALLOW TO COOL BEFORE SERVING IT TO YOUR PET

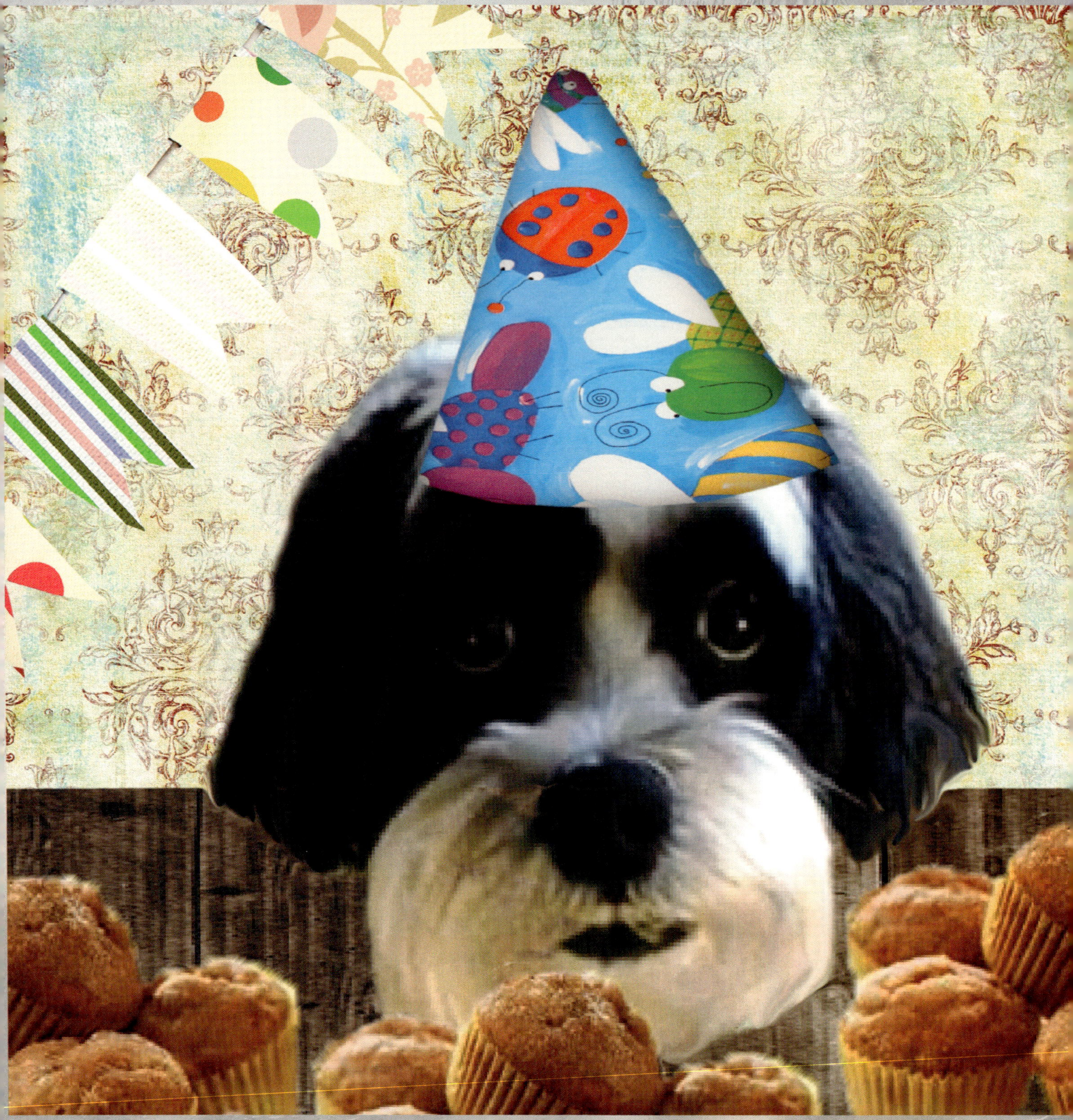

CELEBRATION MUFFINS

INGREDIENTS

1 small banana, 100g rice flour, 30g grated almonds, 1.5 tsp baking powder, 50g low fat natural yoghurt, 1 egg, 1 tsp coconut oil and a sprinkle of cinnamon.

INSTRUCTIONS

Peel your banana. Mash it up in a small bowl using a fork.

Mix in the flour, the grated almonds and the baking powder all together. Now add in your egg and coconut oil, cinnamon plus 175ml of warm water.

Blend all of your ingredients together until all of the dry ingredients are moist.

Add paper cases to your muffin tin and fill each one 3/4 full with the mixture.

Cook in a pre-heated oven at 392F for 20-25 minutes.

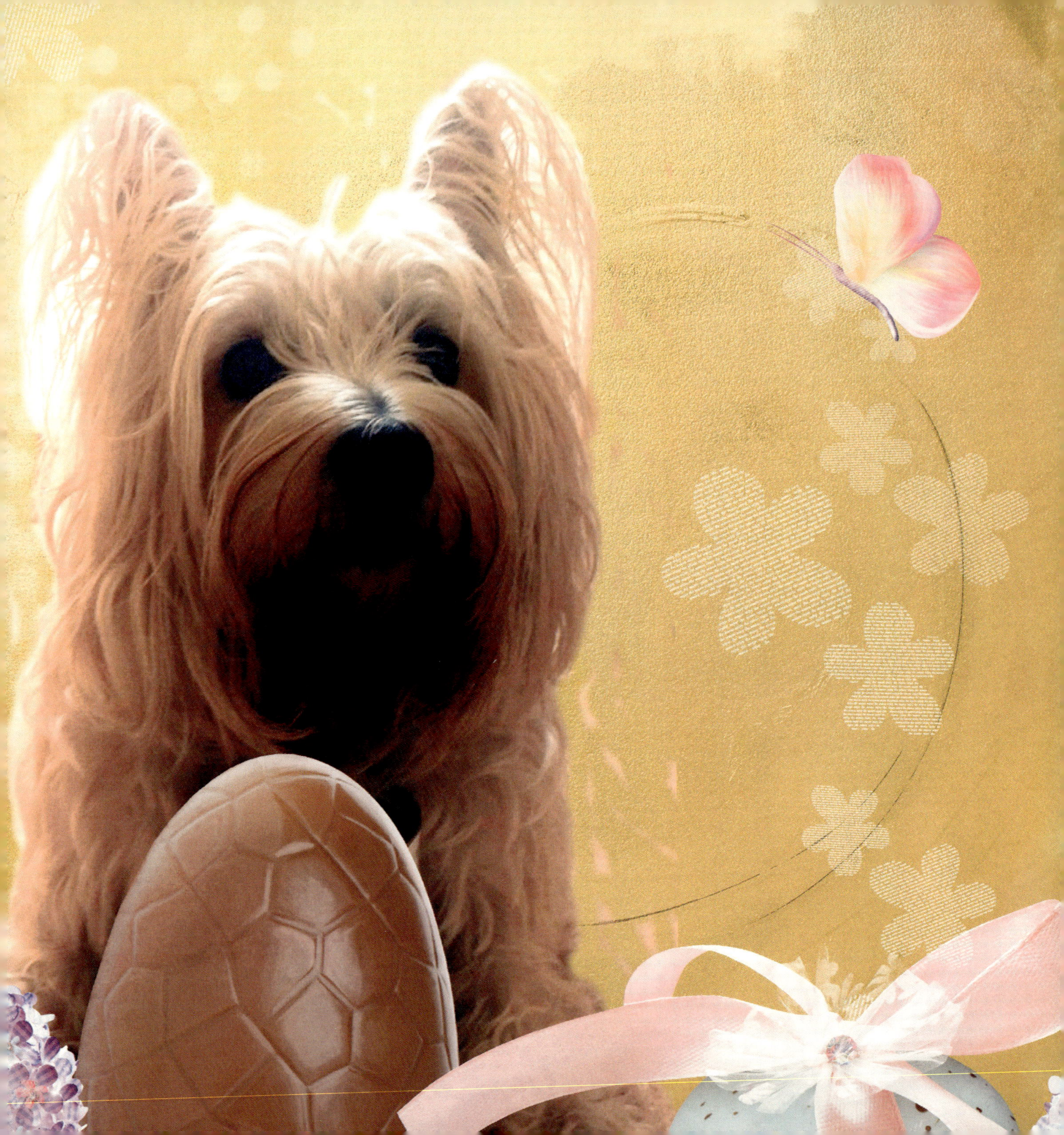

DOG FRIENDLY EASTER EGG

Do not be tempted to share your human grade chocolate with your canine friend as chocolate can be highly toxic to dogs.

INGREDIENTS

Several packets of doggy choc drops, an Easter egg mould, a small saucepan, a bowl and spoons.

INSTRUCTIONS

Place the chocolate drops into a heatproof bowl.
Fill the saucepan with water and place the bowl on top.
Warm the water gradually and stir the melting chocolate.
Lightly grease the egg mould and spoon the melted chocolate evenly around it. Place the mould in the fridge.

Once the two halves have set, fill one half with some of your dogs favourite treats. Spread melted chocolate around the edge of one half of the egg and stick the second half in place. Once cool, trim away any rough edges and wrap the egg in cellophane and tie with a pretty ribbon to secure.

ONLY FEED YOUR DOG A SMALL AMOUNT AT A TIME

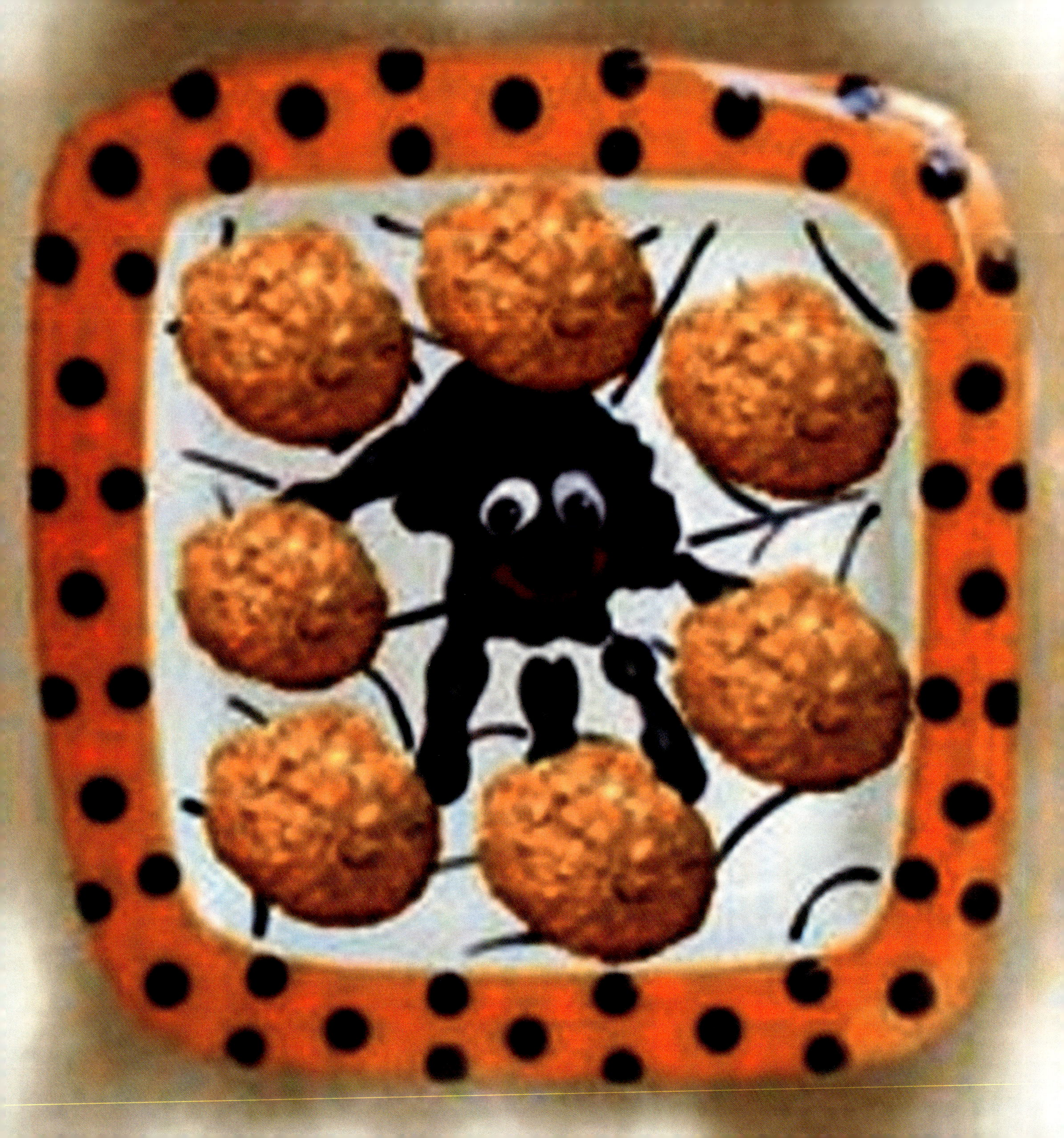

Pumpkin Balls

MIX TOGETHER IN A MIXING BOWL

2 cups of oat flour, 1 egg, 1 cup of mashed pumpkin, 2 tablespoons of honey, 2 teaspoons of ground flax seeds, 1/4 teaspoon cinnamon 1/4 teaspoon sea salt.

Leave the mixture to chill for 30 minutes in the refridgerator then shape the mixture into balls and place them onto a lined baking tray.

COOK IN THE OVEN AT 350 DEGREES FOR 20 MINUTES

Remove them from the oven and allow them to cool. To make them crispier, return them back to the oven and cook them for a further 20 minutes.

THESE TREATS HAVE A CRISPY OUTSIDE AND A SOFT MOIST CENTRE.

THEY SHOULD BE KEPT IN THE REFRIGERATOR AND CONSUMED WITHIN ONE WEEK.

JOY
LOVE
PEACE
REJOICE
TOGETHER
CHRISTMAS

DOG FRIENDLY CHRISTMAS PUDDING

INGREDIENTS

110g vegetable suet, 100g self-raisng flour (sifted), 150g white breadcrumbs, 1/2 tsp cinnamon, 1/2 tsp ginger, a pinch of ground cloves, a sprinkle of nutmeg, 50g blackstrap molasses, 100g runny honey, 100g blackcurrants (not currants as these are highly toxic to dogs). 50g dried cranberries, 50g skinned and chopped almonds, 1 grated pear or apple, the juice and the zest of one lemon, 3 free-range eggs and 150ml of milk.

INSTRUCTIONS

Place flour into a mixing bowl and sift in all spices and seasoning. Mix in the remainder of the dry ingredients. Beat in the eggs, mix in the lemon juice and other liquids. After adding all ingredients you need to blend the mixture very well. It should be light brown and fairly sloppy in texture. You can add a little extra milk, should it require thinning out. Test it by taking a spoonful and then allowing it to drop off the spoon and back into the bowl.

Compress the mixture in order to release any air pockets then leave it to sit for a few hours in a covered mixing bowl in order to give the dried fruit and breadcrumbs time to absorb the liquid.

For the mould, you will need a 1.2 litre glass pudding bowl with a rim. Place the mixture in the bowl. Cover with a sheet of greaseproof paper and a sheet of foil then tie securely with string. Place in a steamer over a pan of hot water and steam for 5-6 hours. Checking and topping up the boiling water as needed.

TO REHEAT ON CHRISTMAS DAY, STEAM IT FOR A FURTHER 3 HOURS.

Treats

Menu

TEMPTING TREATS

Tuna Crunchies
Museli Munchies
Beefy Bites
Turkey Nibbles
Sausage Surprise
Veggie Canine Crisps
Pizzeria Starletta
Little Starlett's Big Star

♥

TUNA CRUNCHIES

INGREDIENTS

1 can (5 ounces) of tuna packed in brine,
1 large egg, 1 tablespoon of olive oil,
1 heaped tablespoon of dried catnip,
1 teacup of oat flour.

INSTRUCTIONS

Preheat your oven to 350 degrees F, then line your baking tray with greaseproof paper for later.

Drain the water from the tuna and mix in a bowl together with the oat flour, egg, olive oil and the catnip. Blend it until the mixture is smooth.

Roll into small balls and place them onto the greaseproof paper. Mark them with an X shape using the side of a skewer.

Bake for 10-12 minutes and allow to cool before serving. Store in an airtight container in the refridgerator for up to seven days.

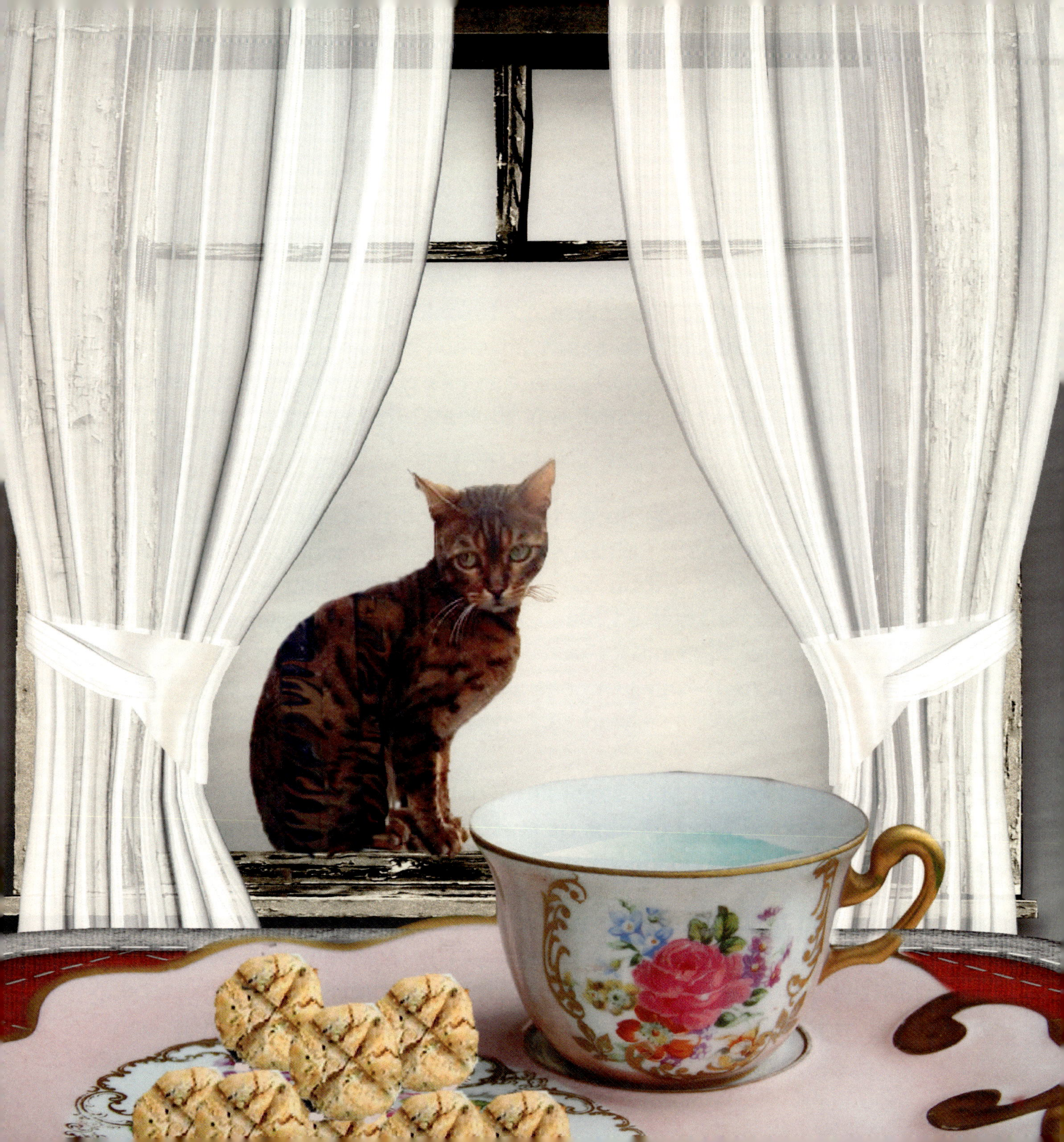

Bon Appétit

STARLETT''S
SECRET
COCONUT OIL

MUSELI MUNCHIES

INGREDIENTS

300g museli (mixed grain)
80g cornflakes
600g spelt flour
400ml water
2 tablespoons of coconut oil
2 eggs

INSTRUCTIONS

Preheat your oven to 170°C

In a large mixing bowl, mix together the 400ml of water, coconut oil and eggs. Add in the museli, cornflakes and flour and knead all of the ingredients together into a firm mixture.

Flour your worktop and then roll your dough out to 7mm in thickness. Score the dough into bite-sized segments. Bake in the oven for 40 minutes. Cut into segments, alow to stand for an hour to dry out and get crispy. Store in an air-tight container for 3 weeks.

BEEFY BITES

INGREDIENTS

1lb (500g) lean beef

INSTRUCTIONS

Dice the beef into half inch (1cm) cubes.

Cover a baking tray with greaseproof paper and place the cubes of meat on it closely together.

Place into a cold oven and heat to 300F and cook for one hour. Reduce the temperature to 210F and prop open the oven door to allow the moisture to escape. Cook on this lower heat for a further 2 hours. Allow the beefy bites to dry overnight at room temperature so they become crispy and crunchy.

STORE IN AN AIRTIGHT CONTAINER FOR 3 MONTHS IF YOUR DOG WILL ALLOW.

TURKEY NIBBLES

INGREDIENTS

160g lean minced turkey, 40g potatoes, 75g carrots, 50g corn flour, 1 egg, 1/2 teaspoon garlic powder, 1 tsp vegetable oil, flour for dusting your work surface.

INSTRUCTIONS

Wash and finely grate your carrots and place in a mixing bowl. Add in all of your dry ingredients followed by your wet ingredients and blend all together very well to form a dough. Wrap the dough in tin foil and store it overnight in your refrigerator.

Lighty dust your work surface with the flour and then, using your hands, carefully press the crumbly biscuit dough onto a flat surface to approximately 1.5cm thick. Cut the dough into squares and transfer all onto a baking tray lined with greaseproof paper and bake at 482F for 30 minutes or so. Or until they are golden brown.

To make them extra crunchy reduce the oven temperature to 167F and bake for 4 hours or until hard. Leave to air-dry for 24 hours.

STORE IN AN AIR-TIGHT CONTAINER FOR UP TO 3 MONTHS

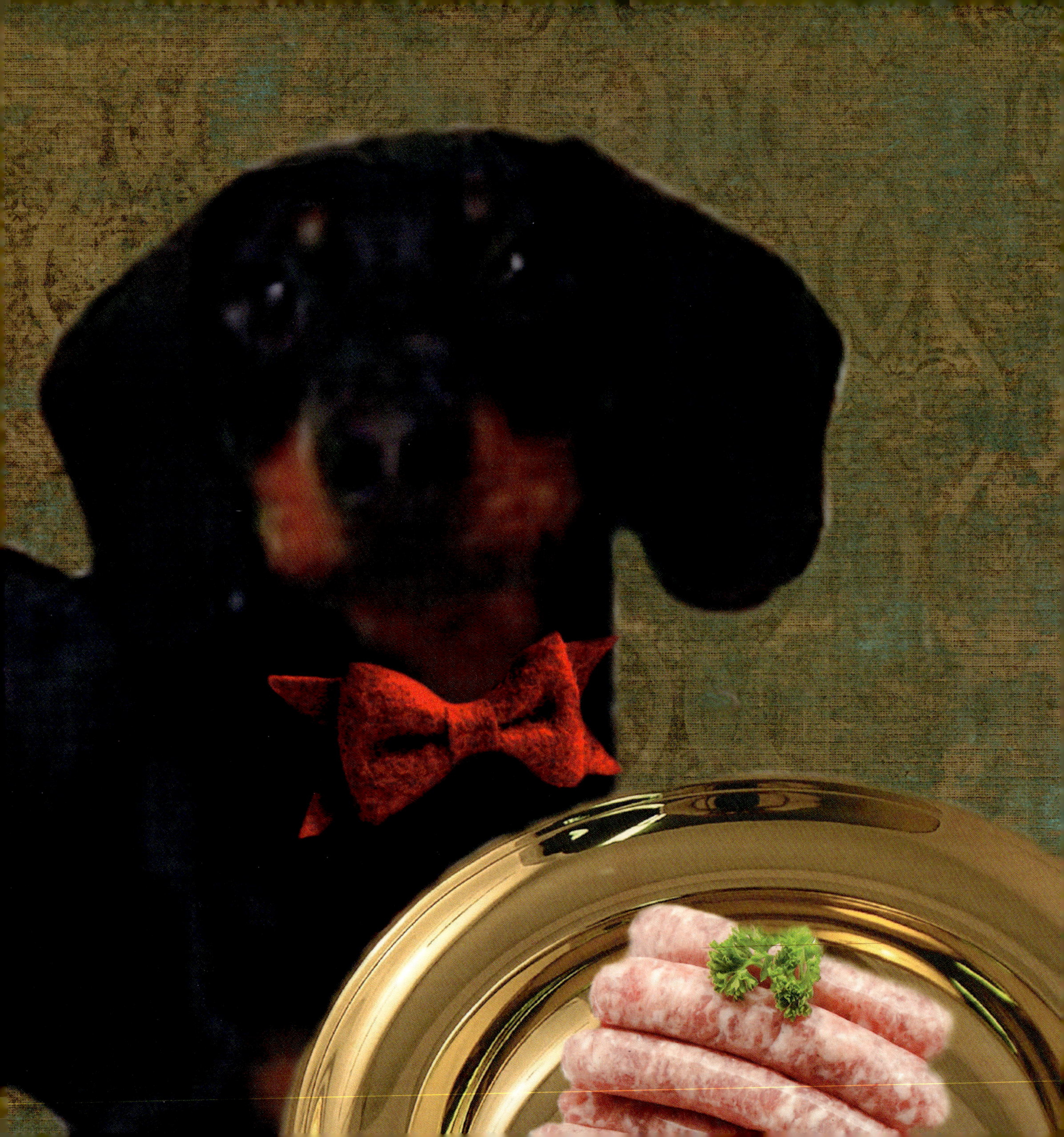

SAUSAGE SURPRISE

INGREDIENTS

100g sausage meat, 1/2 a teacup of flour, 1 egg
1 teaspoon of coconut oil and some mixed herbs.

INSTRUCTIONS

Cut your sausage meat up into bite-sized pieces and mix it together well with all of the other ingredients.

Using a teaspoon, transfer one spoonful of the mixture at a time onto a baking tin which has been lined with greaseproof paper.

Cook in a preheated oven for 25 minutes at 302F

ALLOW TO COOL FOR 30 MINUTES BEFORE SERVING ANY TO YOUR DOG!

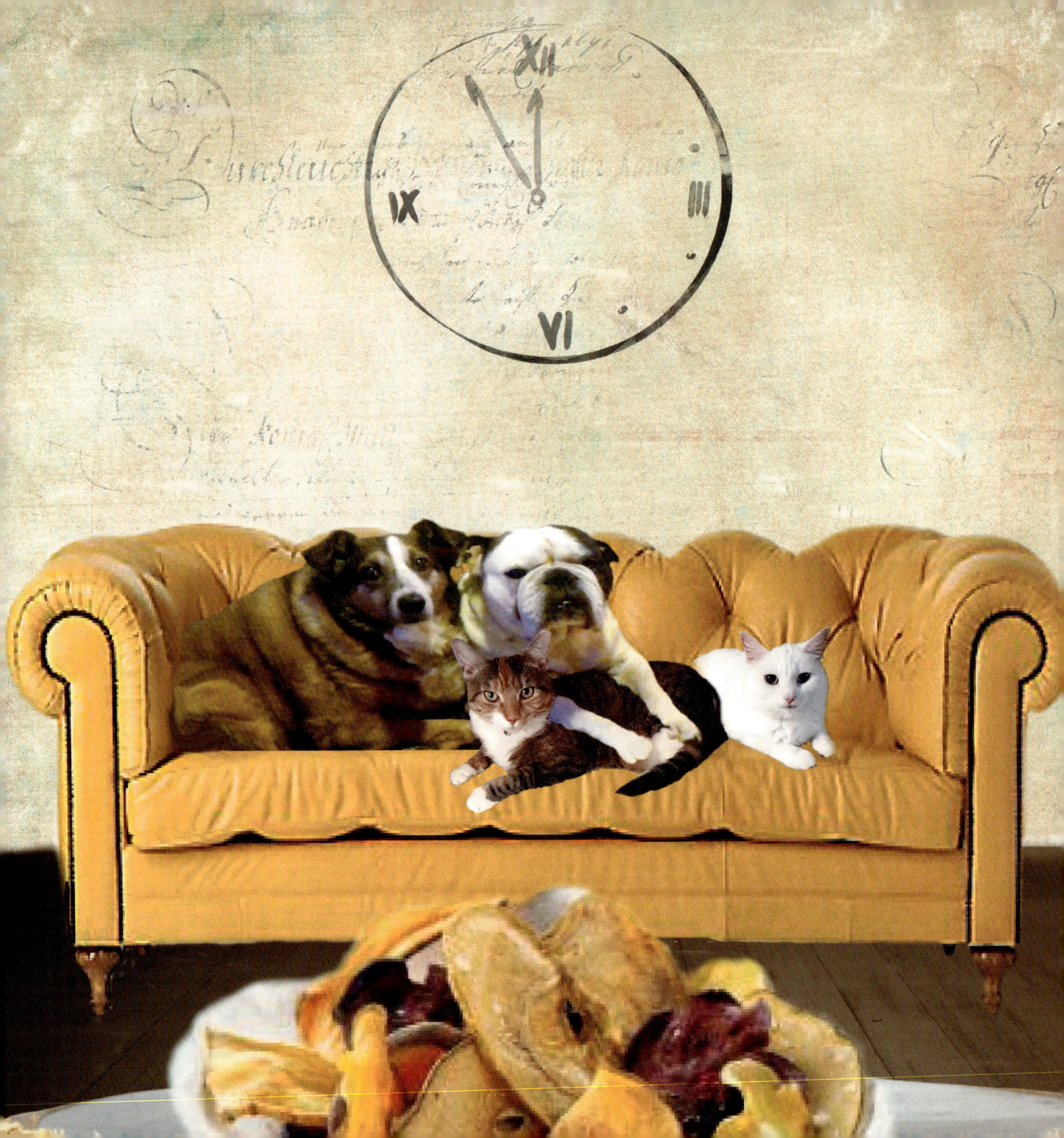

VEGGIE CANINE CRUNCHIES

INGREDIENTS

1 carrot (or 1 apple, 1 banana, or 1 sweet potato).
1 zucchini, 2 eggs, 1 1/4 cups of wholewheat flour,
3 tablespoons of unsalted un-shelled sunflower seeds
1 tablespoon of sunflower oil and 1 tablespoon of milk

INSTRUCTIONS

Preheat your oven to 350 F

Finely grate your chosen fruit or vegetable into a mixing bowl. Add in the sunflower seeds, sunflower oil and the 2 eggs. Add in the flour, milk and mixed herbs and knead all into a firm dough.

Take teaspoon sized amounts of the mixture and roll into balls. Using the back of your teaspoon, flatten the balls into crisp like shapes.

Bake for 20-25 minutes, turn off your oven and allow the crisps dry in the oven overnight.

* Cats by nature are carnivores but may enjoy these with added catnip *

Pizzeria Starletta

INGREDIENTS

70g lean minced beef
200g wholewheat flour
50g mozzarella cheese
3 tbsp vegetable oil
10g fresh yeast

INSTRUCTIONS

Preheat your oven to 375 F

Pour flour into a mixing bowl.

Make a small well in the centre.

Dissolve the yeast in 80ml of warm water, then pour the mixture into the well and mix with a little bit of flour. Then pour in the oil.

Mix all ingredients together. Knead into a firm dough. Pull off small amounts. Using a star shaped cutter, cut out star shapes then flatten them out using a rolling pin. Add topping of mince and mozzerella. Sprinkle on mixed herbs. Bake on tray for 20 minutes.

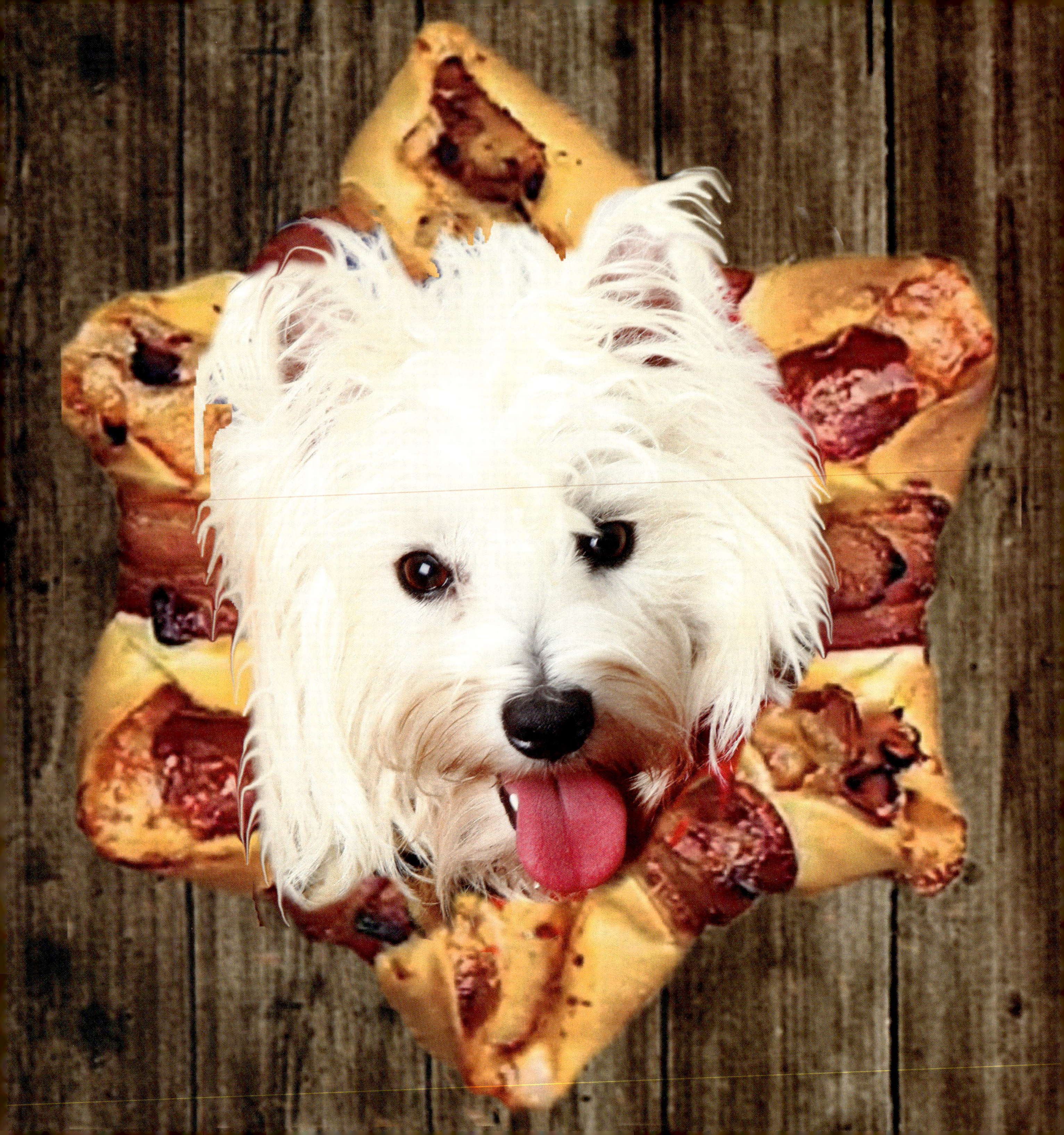

LITTLE STAR'S BIG STAR

INGREDIENTS

1 sheet of ready made puff pastry, tomato puree, grated cheese, 6 slices of streaky bacon, 2 salami slices, diced ham and chicken, Add a sprinkle of mixed herbs to season.

INSTRUCTIONS

Cut out a circle using a plate, then cut lines.

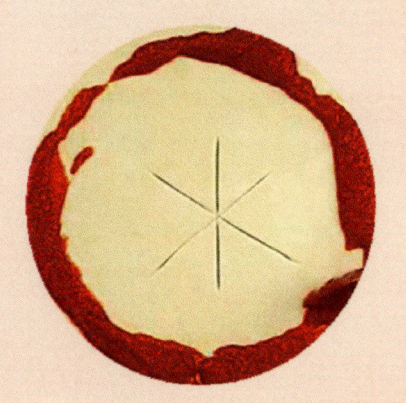

Add tomato puree to edges.

Sprinke on the grated cheese.

Roll the edges inward and the centres outwards.

To look like this.

Wrap the streaky bacon around. Fill with meats.

Cook for 25 minutes at 400 F

English Breakfast
TEA
a blend of fine tea producing
a distinctive English brew
Net Wt. 3 ozs.

KEEP CALM AND *drink tea*

HEALTHY HERBAL TEA

There are some herbal teas which are believed to produce the same positive health benefits in dogs as they do in humans. These benefits include an improved immune system, improved energy, anti-inflammatory properties, detoxification, and more.

Throughout history herbal teas have long been considered a means of improving both body and mind. Healers have noted the positive health effects and have shared their information in numerous cultures.

Nowadays many people continue to enjoy herbal teas for their distinct fragrances and flavors, as well as their naturally beneficial qualities. Many herbal teas contain antioxidants, and some studies have shown a correlation between the consumption of antioxidant-rich foods and a lowered risk for certain neurological disorders, cancers, and heart disease in individuals. In terms of their therapeutic properties, many teas are believed to improve a number of negative conditions, ranging from upset stomach to bad breath and sleeping trouble.

Some herbal teas are believed to produce the same positive health benefits in dogs as they do in humans.
Since dogs truly are a human's best friend, it makes perfect sense for us to share healthy herbal teas with them.

TEAS WHICH CAN BENEFIT YOUR DOGS HEALTH

CHAMOMILE

calms the stomach, heals skin problems,
strenghtens the muscles of the heart and the bladder

COCONUT

aids the brain, skin, hair, nails, teeth, cholesterol
burns off fat, kills bacteria, viruses and fungi.

DANDELION

a natural diuretic to aid urine infections by expelling toxins

ECHINACEA

aids the immune system by fighting bacteria and viruses
check with your Vet as some dogs may be allergic to this.

GINGER

aids stomach disorders and can stop vomitting.
use in small portions. (3 slices to one teacup.)

"THE PERFECT BREW WILL SEE YOU THROUGH"

Place one bag of your chosen herbal tea into a glass measuring jug. (Not plastic as plastics release carcinogens when heated).

Pour in 8.5 floz of boiling water and leave it to brew for about 5 minutes before removing the teabag. Now thoroughly stir it up.

Allow the tea to cool to room temperature. (Dogs should never ever consume hot tea as it can seriously burn or injure them.)

Once the tea is cool do not add any sugar or artifical sweetners as many including xylitol are poisonous to pets. Instead add in a light drizzle of raw honey.

THIS WAY
TO THE
MAD HATTER'S
TEA PARTY
☞

STARLETT'S
WESTIE
TEA PARTY

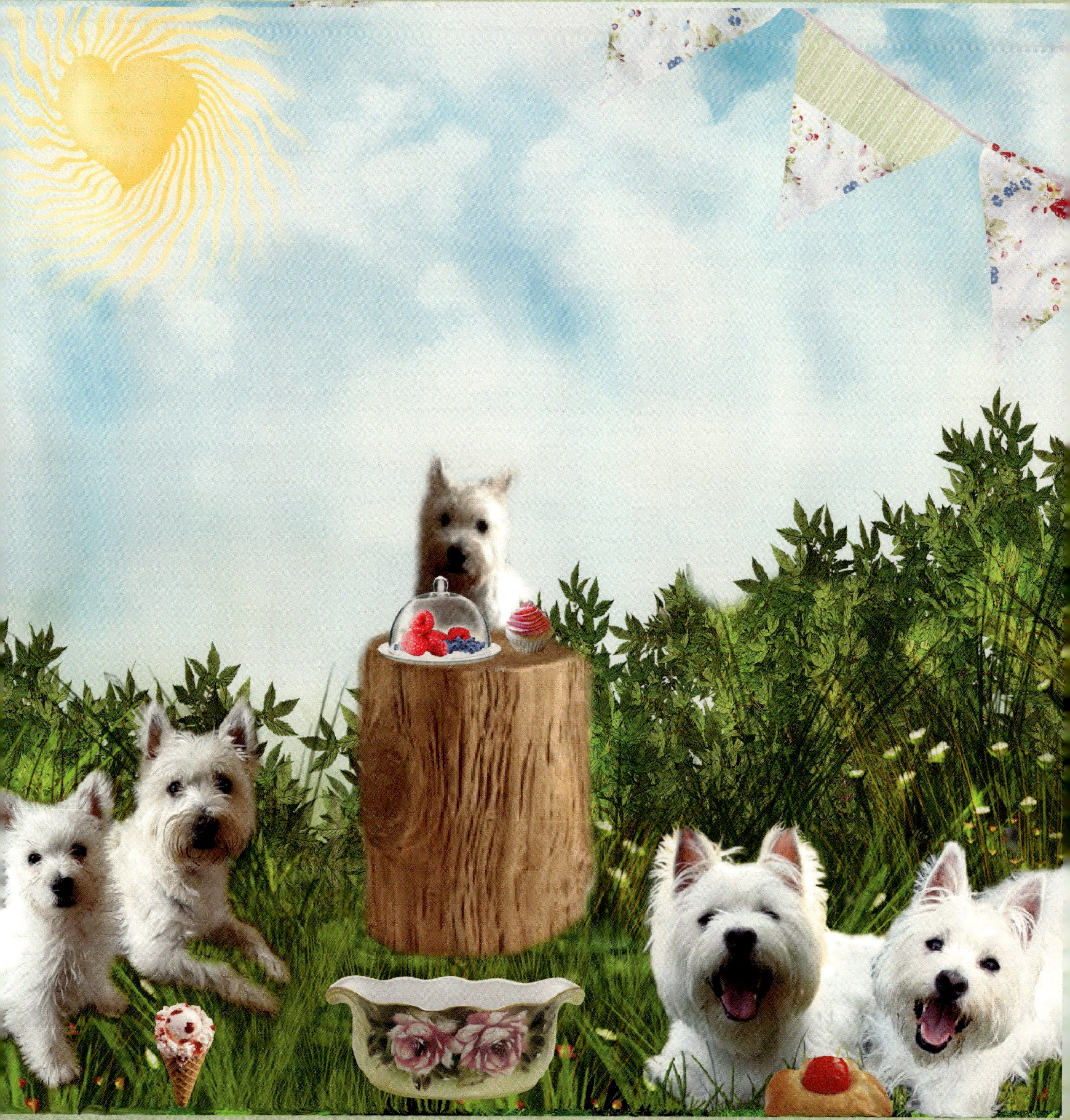

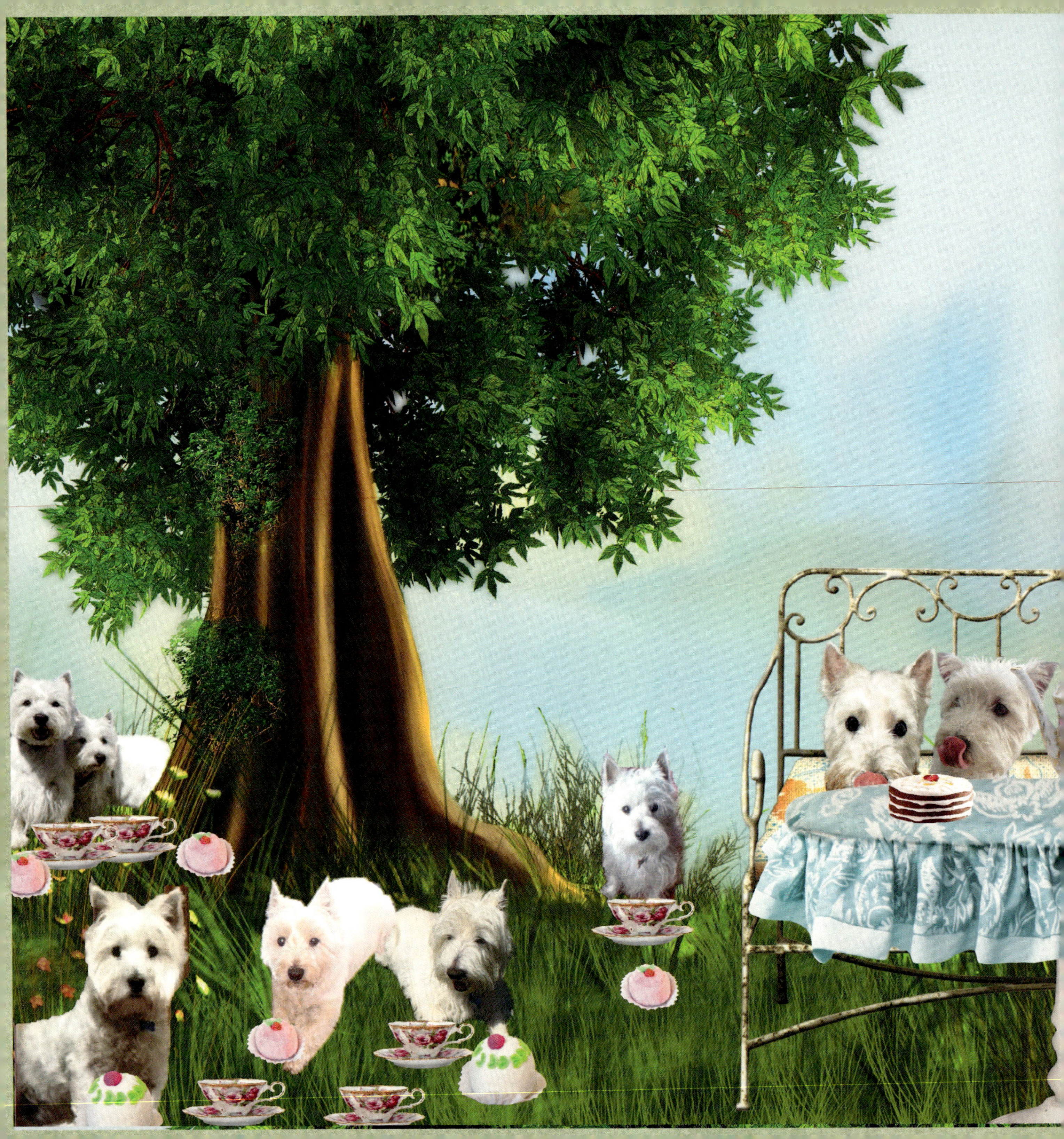

STARLETT'S WESTIE TEA PARTY

This kitchen is Seasoned with Love

Menu

FEELING PAWLY?

Constipation: Almond Bran Biscuits

Convalescents: Chicken Broth Soup
Chicken and Oatmeal Bowl

Dehydration: Tuna Melts
Fruit and Veg Pupsicles

Dental: Teeth Cleaning Biscuits
Breath~freshening Treats

Fur Conditioning: Fruit & Veggie Surprise

Nourishment: Marvellous Mashed Potato

Weight Watchers Platter

Wind Crunchies & A Fresh Breeze

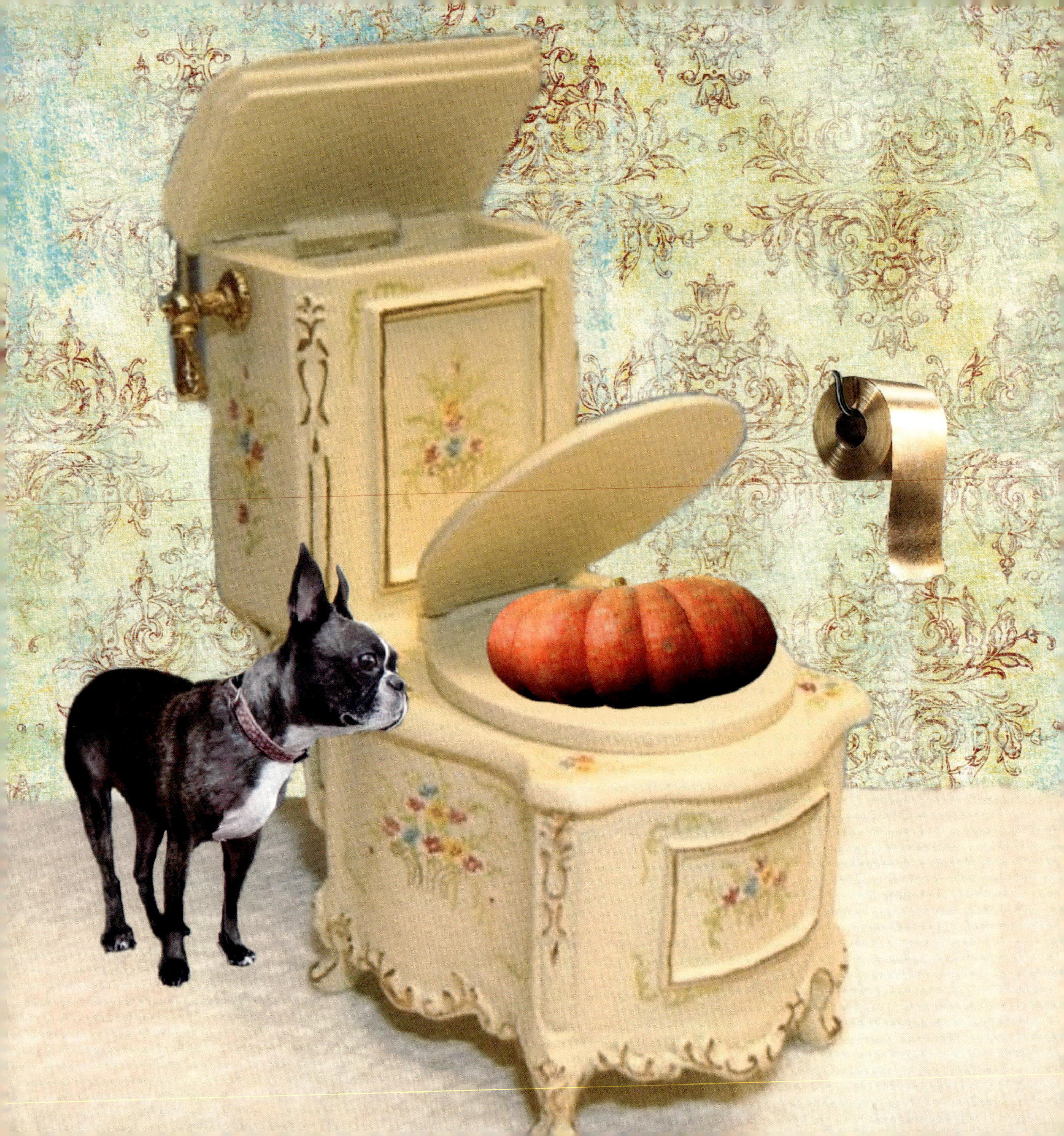

ALMOND BRAN BISCUITS
(helps with constipation)

INGREDIENTS

450g wholemeal flour, 60ml coconut oil, 50g diced pumpkin, 2 tbsp of almond bran, 1 tsp of finely chopped fresh parsley, flour for dusting and milk for glazing.

INSTRUCTIONS

Place the diced pumpkin and the chopped parsley into a blender. Add in the coconut oil. Blend until it is a puree. Pour into a mixing bowl. Add in the flour and the bran and kneadit into a firm dough. If the dough feels too dry add in a little water. Shape the dough into a ball and wrap it in cling film. Place it in the fridge for 30 minutes to set.

Preheat your oven to 320F. Line your baking tray with greaseproof paper.

Roll out the dough 1/4 inch thick and cut out shapes using biscuit cutters. Glaze them with milk and cook for 30 minutes. Allow to cool on a wire rack before sharing one a day with your dog. These can both prevent and aid constipation

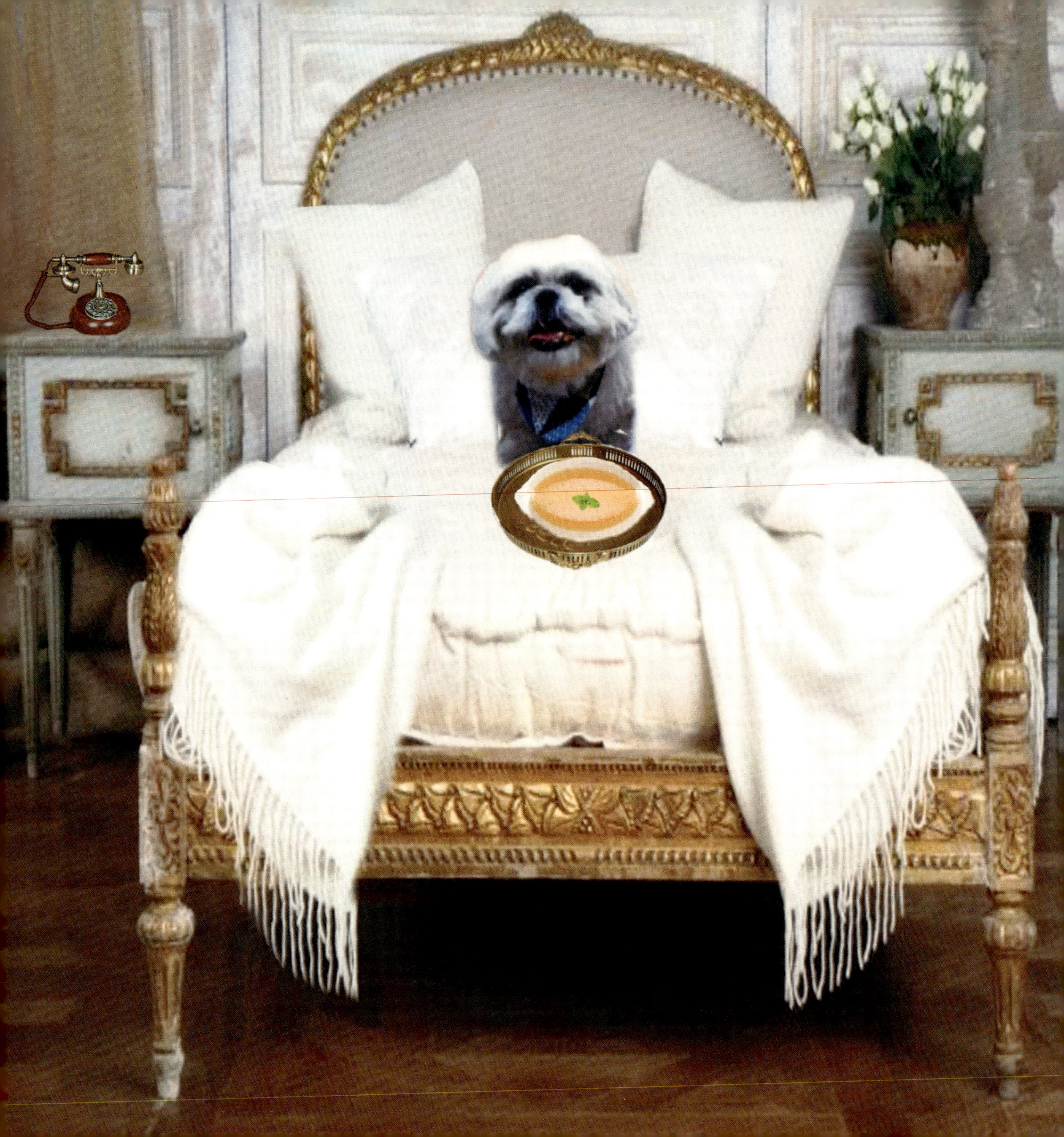

CHICKEN BROTH SOUP
CHICKEN AND OATMEAL BOWL
(for convalescents and strength)

CHICKEN BROTH SOUP
INGREDIENTS

1 whole chicken, cooked, 2 large carrots, 2 large potatoes, water.

INSTRUCTIONS

Remove the skin from the chicken and cut it into pieces. Place it in a large stock pot. Peel and cut carrots and potatoes and add them with the chicken. Pour enough water into the pot to cover all of the ingredients. Cook on high until it comes to a rolling boil. Reduce to a simmer, cover and cook for two hours. Add water if necessary to prevent soup from boiling dry. Remove the pot from the stove and allow it to cool. Once completely cooled, skim any fat off the top. Remove chicken and vegetables and strain the broth to remove any debris.

CHICKEN AND OATMEAL BOWL
INGREDIENTS

1 whole chicken, 150g fine porridge oats, 1 carrot, 1 celery stick, 1tsp chopped parsley

INSTRUCTIONS

In 4 pints of water cook the chicken and mixed vegetables for 1.5 hours. Discard the vegetables. Remove the chicken from the stock and allow to cool. Skim of any fat in the stock. Skin and bone the chicken. Cut the meat into small pieces. Stir the oats into 2 pints of the stock and bring to the boil. Allow it to thicken, stirring for 2 minutes before removing it from the heat. Mix this thin porridge in with the chicken meat.

SERVE AT ROOM TEMPERATURE

TUNA MELTS
(prevent dehydration)

INGREDIENTS

1 can low sodium green string beans and 1 can tuna packed in brine

INSTRUCTIONS

Drain both cans and thoroughly mix together the string beans and tuna. Form into bite-sized balls, squeezing out excess liquid in the process.

This should make 12-14 balls.

Place all balls onto a tray or a plate lined with tin foil or greaseproof paper.

Place in the freezer for about one hour.

Remove the amount you wish to serve, (just a couple at a time per dog or cat) and serve immediately.

THESE CAN BE STORED IN THE FREEZER FOR UP TO 3 MONTHS, BUT SHOULD BE DEFROSTED TO A CRUNCHY TEXTURE BEFORE SERVING.

FRUIT AND VEG PUPSICLES
(prevent dehydration)

INGREDIENTS

Dog friendly fruits, vegetables, with apple juice or fresh meat with herbs and meat stock. Plastic lolly moulds. Halfed down the middle carrots for sticks.

INSTRUCTIONS

Place your chosen combination of the above ingredients into your plastic lolly moulds.

Pour in the apple juce with the fruits or vegetables.

Pour in the meat stock and add in the herbs with the fresh meat.

Place in the freezer. After one hour (when partly set) add in the carrot leaving a couple of inches poking out at the top to be used as a handle. Place back in the freezer until fully frozen.

DOGS SHOULD BE SUPERVISED WHILST ENJOYING THESE!

TEETH CLEANING BISCUITS

INGREDIENTS

1/4 cup honey, 1.5 cups whole wheat flour, 1 cup white flour, 1/2 cup cornmeal, 1/4 cup spinach powder, 1/2 cup oats 1/4 cup bran, 1 tbsp bone meal, 1.5 tsp baking powder, 1 1/2 cups water, 1 teaspoon peppermint extract.

INSTRUCTIONS

In a large mixing bowl, mix in together all of the dry ingredients, then add in the wet.

Roll out and each ball your dough and using biscuit cutters, cut out your biscuits to approximately 1.5cm thickness.

Cook at 300F for 35 minutes (or until golden brown).

ALLOW TO DRY OUT AND HARDEN OVERNIGHT.

STORE IN AN AIR-TIGHT TIN.

BREATH FRESHENING TREATS

INGREDIENTS

200g whole wheat flour
fresh Parsley
fresh Mint
(or pure mint extract)
1 egg
20g coconut oil

INSTRUCTIONS

Mix all ingredients together. Roll out the dough to 1.5 cm in thickness. Cut out shapes using biscuit cutters.

Cook at 300F for 35 minutes (until golden brown.)

STORE IN AN AIR-TIGHT TIN.

FRUIT AND VEGGIE SURPRISE
(fur conditioning)

INGREDIENTS

1 apple, 1 banana, 2 carrots, 100ml unsalted chicken stock 200g porridge oats, 20g coconut oil, 1 hard boiled egg, 1 tbsp of finely chopped mixed herbs.

INSTRUCTIONS

Puree the apple, banana, carrots and chicken stock in a blender.

Then mix it all in well with the oats, and the coconut oil.

Divide the mixture into small portions.

Peel and chop the hard boiled egg.

After placing each portion in your dog's bowl, add in both a sprinkling of the egg and the mixed herbs.

STORE IN THE REFRIDGERATOR FOR 3 DAYS. SERVE AT ROOM TEMPERATURE.

MARVELLOUS MASHED POTATO
(nourishment)

INGREDIENTS

300g chicken breast, 500g potatoes, 100g cottage cheese

INSTRUCTIONS

Slice the chicken breast into small bite-sized chunks and cook for 25 minutes in 2 pints of water. Once cooked, remove from the stock and allow to cool.

Boil the potatoes in their skins in unsalted water until soft.

Drain off the water and peel them.

Using some of the chicken stock make a soft mash.

Mix in the chicken and the cottage cheese.

STORE IN THE REFRIDGERATOR. SERVE IN SMALL PORTIONS AT ROOM TEMPERATURE

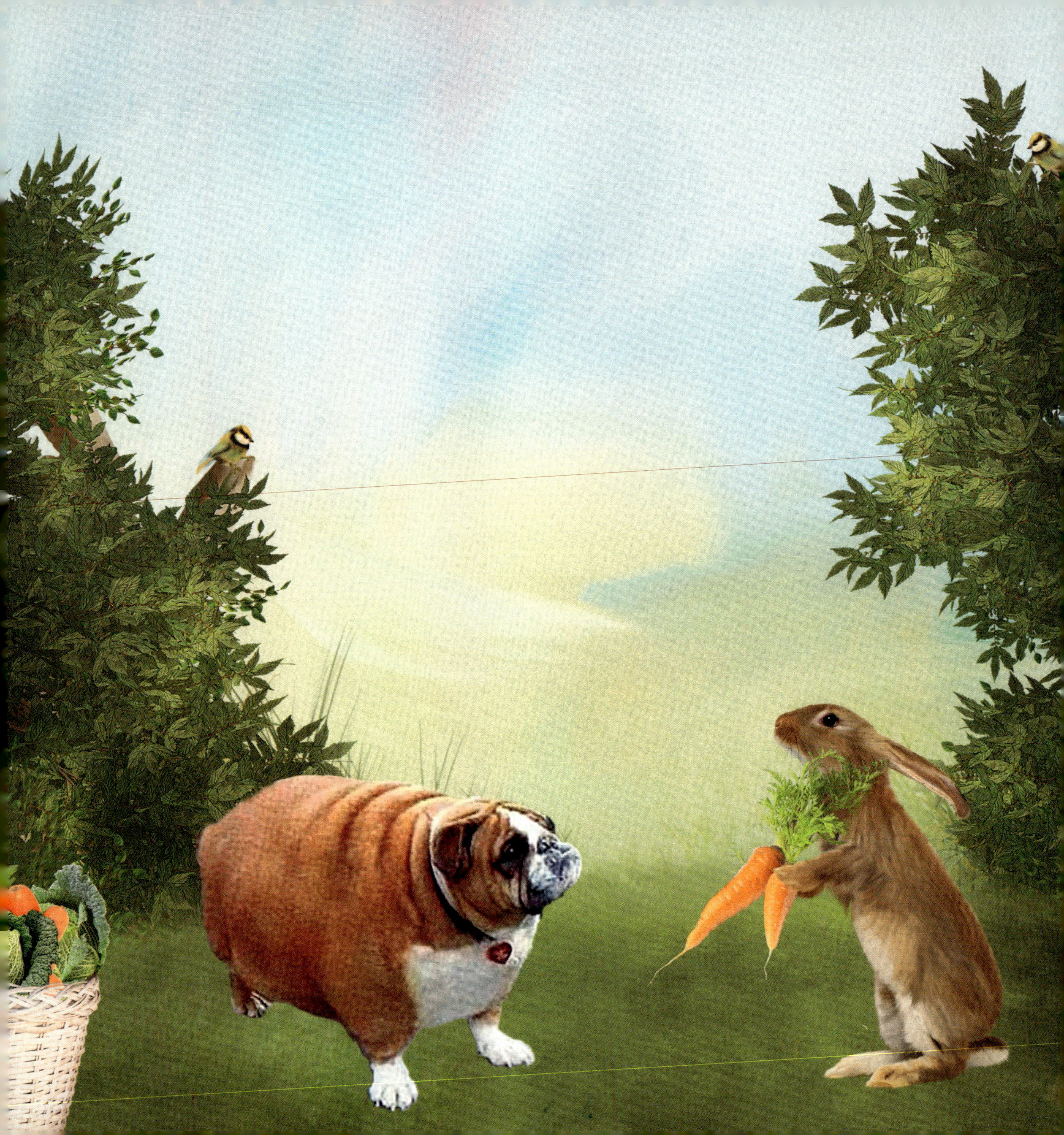

WEIGHT WATCHER'S PLATTER

INGREDIENTS

7oz (200g) of lean organic beef

7oz (200g) of each: grated carrot, bean sprouts & celery

7oz (200g) cooked bran

3.5oz (100g) low-fat natural yogurt

1 tablespoon of sunflower oil

INSTRUCTIONS

Cut the beef into small square pieces and brown in a non-stick pan with the sunflower oil.

Cut the celery up into thin strips and together with the grated carrot add both to the meat.

Add in a little water, simmer for 15 minutes, allow to cool. Stir in chopped bean sprouts and bran. Drain the used water into the low-fat yogurt and drizzle it over the food.

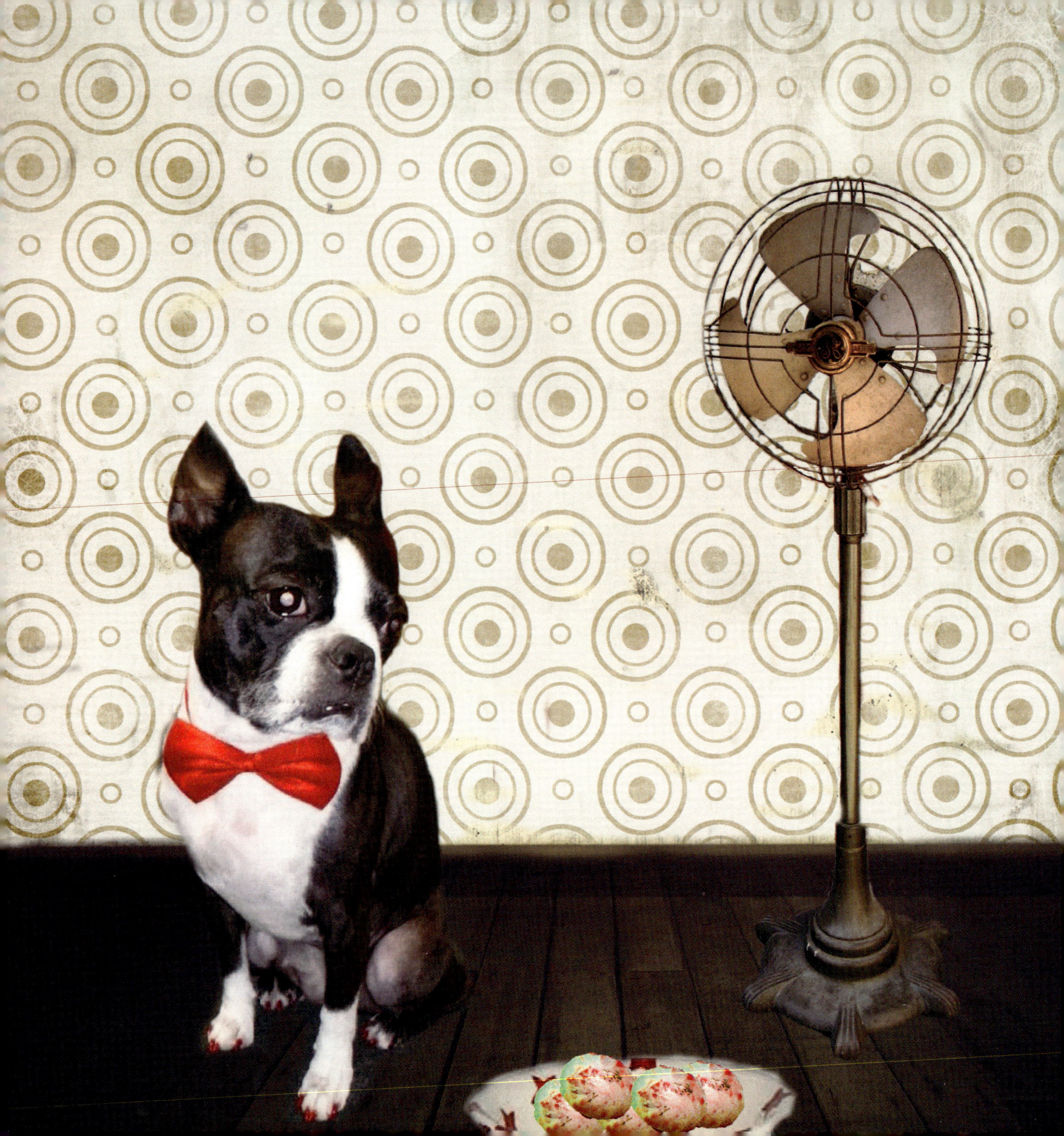

WIND CRUNCHIES & A FRESH BREEZE

WIND CRUNCHIES - INGREDIENTS

250g gluten-free flour, 1 egg, 3tbsp olive oil, 125ml skimmed milk 1 tsp finely chopped mint and parsley.

INSTRUCTIONS

Mix the flour, egg, olive oile and milk to make a pliable dough. Mix in the chopped herbs.

Place portions of the dough into an icing bag with a star top and squeeze out different biscuit shapes onto a lined baking tray.

BAKE AT 345F FOR 15-20 MINUTES. DRY IN THE OVEN FOR AN HOUR.

A FRESH BREEZE - INGREDIENTS

150g instant polenta, 1tbsp corn oil, 125ml unsalted chicken stock, 1 egg, 1tbsp grated parmesan cheese and 2 tbsp finely chopped mint.

In a bowl mix together the polenta with the oil. In a pan bring the chicken stock to the boil and stir in the polenta/oil mixture.
Allow it to thicken for a few minutes, whilst stirring.
Knead the remaining ingredients into the polenta.
Shape into walnut sized balls and place on a baking sheet.

BAKE AT 345F FOR 40 MINUTES
ALLOW TO DRY IN THE OVEN FOR AN HOUR.

USEFUL INFORMATION

Temperature
{Conversion} = {Chart}

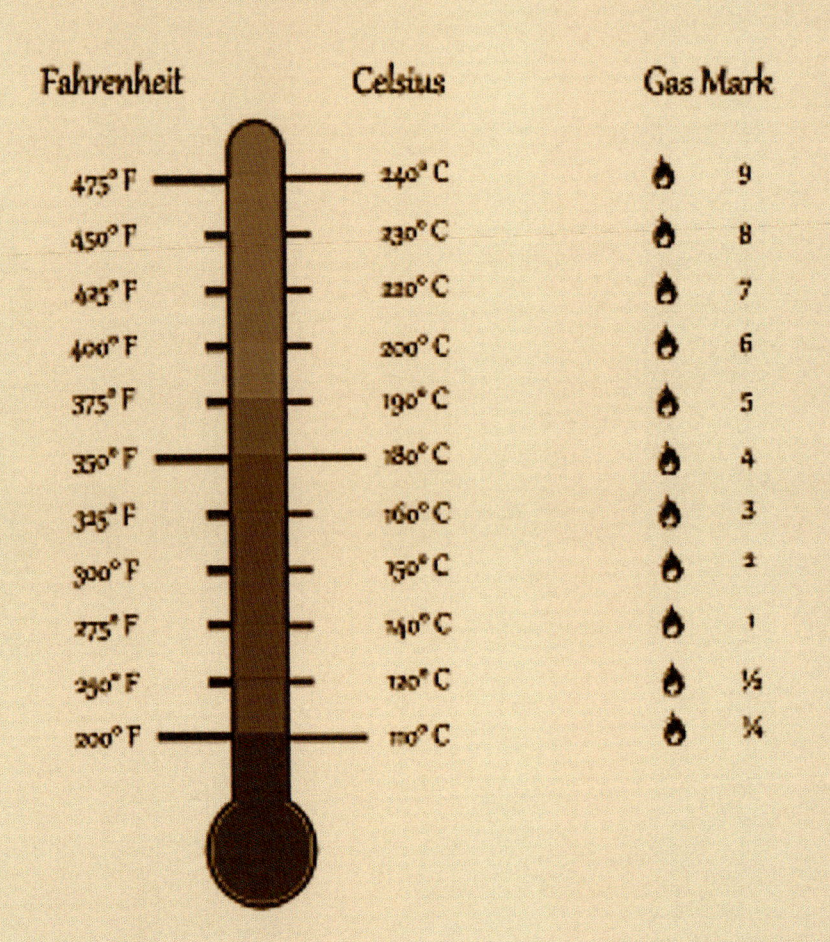

Fahrenheit	Celsius	Gas Mark
475° F	240° C	9
450° F	230° C	8
425° F	220° C	7
400° F	200° C	6
375° F	190° C	5
350° F	180° C	4
325° F	160° C	3
300° F	150° C	2
275° F	140° C	1
250° F	120° C	½
200° F	110° C	¼

Metric	Imperial	American
5 ml	1/6 fl oz	1 teaspoon
10 ml	1/3 fl oz	1 dessertspoon
15 ml	1/2 fl oz	1 tablespoon
60 ml	2 fl oz	1/4 cup (4 tablespoons)
85 ml	2 1/2 fl oz	1/3 cup
90 ml	3 fl oz	3/8 cup (6 tablespoons)
125 ml	4 fl oz	1/2 cup
180 ml	6 fl oz	3/4 cup
250 ml	8 fl oz	1 cup
300 ml	10 fl oz (1/2 pint)	1 1/4 cups
375 ml	12 fl oz	1 1/2 cups
435 ml	14 fl oz	1 3/4 cups
500 ml	16 fl oz	2 cups
625 ml	20 fl oz (1 pint)	2 1/2 cups
750 ml	24 fl oz (1 1/5 pints)	3 cups
1 litre	32 fl oz (1 3/5 pints)	4 cups
1.25 litres	40 fl oz (2 pints)	5 cups
1.5 litres	48 fl oz (2 2/5 pints)	6 cups
2.5 litres	80 fl oz (4 pints)	10 cups

We sincerely hope you and your pets enjoy our recipes.
Much love, Louise and Starlett